BS"D

With the help of God

BORN TO SERVE

A SURPRISING APPROACH TO ACHIEVING FULFILMENT IN YOUR LIFE WITH ASTOUNDING INSIGHTS INTO HEALING AND HAPPINESS

SARAH TELESHEVSKY

Your birthday is the day God decided that
the world cannot exist without you.

—The Lubavitcher Rebbe

Contents

FOREWORD

This book was originally intended as a practical guide for parents and teachers, offering a wealth of tools, insights, and vital information to ease their critical journeys and bless them with newfound success. In the process of writing, I had an epiphany: all relationships—familial, professional, social, even spiritual—closely resemble adult-child relationships in many ways, as you will presently discover. Whoever you are and however you occupy yourself, you will find help and healing within these pages, whether or not you live or work with children.

The "G word" has become something to avoid among modern authors. This is unfortunate. By substituting God for nature, chance, or "the Universe," we unwittingly deny our own life force. Please keep an open mind while reading this book. You don't have to believe to benefit, but you may come to see God in a new, intriguing light. This is not a philosophical or religious work; it is a road map to a life of joy, purpose, and fulfilment.

To make reading easier and less cumbersome, I have taken the liberty to use the word "man" when discussing humankind, and either "he" or "she" when sharing ideas or examples. Of course, "man" refers equally to both males and females, as do the many examples and scenarios when I have used either "he" or "she".

The first time you read this book many of the concepts may be unclear or seem rather "esoteric". I recommend that you read the entire book once to familiarize yourself with these concepts and ideas, then read it all the way through a second time. You will find that it will become much clearer and more useful the second time around.

We are all beloved children of the Creator of the universe. Discovering meaning in our lives and growing our own innate gifts will enable us to become true partners in creation. By empowering ourselves, we can inspire our co-inhabitants—and particularly our youth—to become the stewards of the universe we—and they—were born to be.

To life and healing!
Sarah Teleshevsky

ACKNOWLEDGEMENTS

To my dear father, Aron Azriel, son of Moshe Yehuda, may your pure soul rest in peace. You taught me to love and appreciate and embrace every human being and to bring out the best in each person. Daddy, you lived up to your namesake—**Aron,** the High Priest—brother of Moses—who "loved peace, pursued peace, loved all creatures, and brought them close to the holy Torah" (Avoth 1:12); **Azriel**—which means "God is my help." You never forgot that God was constantly by your side, guiding you, assisting you, and prompting you to live your life to the fullest.

To my mother, may you live and be well, for many joyful and fulfilling childhood years! Mummy, you intuitively and wisely introduced me to Haim Ginot when I was barely in my teens, igniting within me a lifelong love of children and education. To Howard Glasser, who taught me the tools of his emotional healing programme—The Nurtured Heart Approach—and who so skilfully and thoroughly illuminated the *energy* factor that made everything else make sense. To the Children's Success Foundation and the entire global Nurtured Heart Approach family for welcoming and accompanying me and countless others on our journeys of self-discovery and healing.

To all my colleagues who challenge, learn with, and teach me. To my students—children and adults—who participate in the dance of life, light, and discovery and continue to create their own steps and rhythm, and their own impact on an ever-changing world. To the authors of the plethora of literature, too many to list, who have all contributed to shaping my understanding of the human phenomena. To the generations of Chassidic Rebbes—and Chabad Rebbes in particular—for guiding me in my growing understanding of this world and of spirituality.

To my children and my children-in-law who love me, challenge me, put up with me, and force me to dig ever deeper in my exploration of the human spirit. To my precious grandchildren, who continually inspire me to do whatever I can to make this world a happier, healthier, and safer place for them to grow up in. To my dear husband, Yisroel, who has constantly and relentlessly supported and encouraged me through my own journey and welcomed me to join him in his.

Special thanks to my dear son Chaim for dedicating many precious hours to proofreading this work and offering invaluable feedback; to the Lubavitcher Rebbe for providing me with specific and very personal guidance every step of the way; and to my Creator, Who made me who I am and to Whom I dedicate this work.

PART 1

ILLUSIONS

A Guide for Parents, Educators, and Mental Health Providers

ILLUSIONS

Today's World Is Full of Illusions

It is the world of smiley faces. Everyone is connected. Everyone is smiling. Everyone is sharing his or her happy moments on popular social media sites. We see the pics; we hear the comments; we like the witticisms, jokes, and cartoons; we enjoy the sharing of news and the novel ability to have our voices heard in ways that weren't even conceived just a decade ago. There is so much information out there; we can Google almost anything and find out all about it. It might seem that we live in a utopian world!

But of course, we know that beneath the surface of the social revolution, life is more complicated and scarier than ever. In spite of being so connected, many people feel lost and lonely. Fear is commonplace, even in relatively safe societies. People are unsure of themselves. They strive to find meaning in their lives. The threat of war is constant, and any war can become global in an instant. We have lost our faith in our governments. World leaders are not qualified to lead; they lack the ability, wisdom, and inclination to protect future generations. For the vast majority, their motivation is only hunger for popularity, power, and prestige. Our planet has no guardians!

On the home front, families are falling apart, and relationships are often shallow and fleeting. We continually face threats to our physical and emotional health and well-being. The daily news is so coloured that it's virtually impossible to separate fact from fiction or wishful thinking. Life has become the quintessential labyrinth.

And yet, it is the human condition to live, love, and procreate. Children coming into the world today may have better odds of surviving childhood, but many are growing up without roots or purpose. They don't know where they came from, why they are here, or where they are going. Parents are at a loss when it comes to childcare, discipline, and direction. Teachers resolutely continue to teach curriculum to children who are increasingly alienated, disenchanted, and apathetic. Is what they learn in school truly relevant to the lives they are going to lead? No one can answer that question.

Nevertheless, it is common practice for parents and teachers to push children to compete aggressively against their peers in school. It is not uncommon for a child's entire childhood to revolve around the competitive, surreal environment of the classroom or sports ground rather than around family and friends. Many children firmly believe that if they are not first or best at *something*, they are failing. Yet school administrations all over the world continue to create policies designed to push their schools into the limelight for producing the highest achievers.

Meanwhile, growing numbers of children are becoming increasingly difficult to manage and motivate. Childhood dysfunction is almost pandemic. Parents, teachers, therapists, and doctors can't keep up.

There is plenty of help freely available, but most of it is conflicting or simply doesn't work in practice. It is an enormous challenge to ensure the healthy development of children in this ever-changing and impossibly complicated world. In spite of all the effort expended to support them, our children are not becoming more self-assured or confident. If anything, they are mentally, spiritually, and emotionally *less* balanced and fulfilled than ever before.

Domestic Crisis

A huge proportion of today's children are growing up in domestic circumstances that are far from ideal. Most parents work and if they are not actually working from home—which is commonplace these days—they are bringing their work home from the office. Many children live in single-parent homes, and even more spend their childhoods being shuttled between the homes of parents who don't get along.

Parents are stressed. Life is difficult, the family unit is crumbling, and there is often no back-up help from grandparents and other extended family. More and more children are left to their own devices when they are not in school, without supervision or assistance with unrealistic homework requirements. Others have demanding after-school commitments which they can't or don't want to give up. Countless children end up in foster care or as wards of the state. Foster children often can't even imagine what a stable family is like!

Government agencies can't cope with the number of families where neglect and/or abuse is suspected or confirmed, and there are not enough resources to support families in crisis. Poverty is on the rise, and unemployment is a real and formidable issue. Drug and alcohol abuse is commonplace.

Professional Crisis

More than a third of all children in the developed world between the ages of eight and adulthood will at some point experience significant feelings of inadequacy and self-doubt—and this is seen as *normal*. In the United States, one in eight children is medicated for some form of mental or emotional dysfunction; countless more are referred for therapy or counselling on a regular basis. In many cases, the therapists these children visit weekly or monthly are themselves searching desperately for new interventions that are more effective.

Teachers burn out more quickly than any other group of professionals. One in three will quit teaching within four years of beginning their careers, despite the fact that they trained as teachers because they really want to work with children!

Behaviour-management programmes don't work. They barely suffice for easy, compliant children and backfire when used with challenging children. In desperation, parents and teachers faithfully follow the guidelines, and when they don't see positive results they unjustly blame themselves. (References: CDC Report: Morbidity and Mortality Weekly Report/Supplements May 17, 2013; NCHS Data Brief September 2008; Mediline

Plus/Healthday June 9, 2016; nami.org, Childhood mental health facts PDF; Child Mind Institute, Childrens Mental Health Report, Speak Up For Kids: Introduction PDF, 2015; NPR.org: the teacher dropout crisis July, 2014; The Atlantic: Why do Teachers Quit? October, 2013; HHS Author Manuscript: Burnout in Mental Health Services September, 2012)

What Is the Problem?

There are very many problems, and some of them are caused by some popular but very disturbing misconceptions.

Misconception Number 1

"The world is doomed to destruction sooner or later, and if there was ever a Creator, He abandoned the world long ago. People must make the most out of a more-or-less hopeless situation, get what they can out of life, and hope that they will stay intact without anything disastrous happening in their lifetimes."

The Facts

Human beings were created to rule over the earth and steward it with wisdom. Our seeming failure to do so will not ever cause God to abandon His handiwork. God created the entire universe with precision and with purpose. Humankind is fulfilling its purpose in this world, either willingly or against its will. This assertion will be discussed at length presently.

Misconception Number 2

"Belief in God is not essential for a person to live a happy, meaningful, and purposeful life, and throughout history, this belief has been a major cause of strife, war, and hatred."

The Facts

Belief in God has never caused strife or political unrest, but the *abuse of religion* certainly has! When a group of people begins to assert that anyone who does not worship or believe as they do is damned, or is less of a person, that group of people has used religion as a pretext for *persecution*.

Misconception Number 3

"It is irresponsible to bring more children into this world until we have solved all the problems of mankind and the world is safe."

The Facts

Children are God's gift to the world. They are our hope and salvation. Our children are the guarantors of the universe. They are the stewards of the earth.

Misconception Number 4

"You were born by accident or by chance."

The Facts

You were born by design. In fact, you were born to serve. Your conception was a deliberate and creative act. Maybe not by your parents, but definitely by your Creator. You were created to leave your own unique, personal footprint on this planet. Your life is a life of service, and you are given a choice: Will you choose to live your life in the service of God and mankind, or will you abuse that gift and choose to serve yourself alone?

Serving only yourself will never bring you happiness. Dedicating yourself to a life of service to God and to the world we share most certainly will.

Misconception Number 5

"The purpose of childhood is to acquire as much formal education as possible, in order to secure a better future."

The Facts

Childhood is the time for acquiring all the skills necessary to negotiate and heal a world in crisis. These include wisdom, understanding and love—for God, mankind, life, nature, and beauty. It's a time to develop a sense of wonder, accountability, and belonging.

All children must be given plenty of opportunities to see themselves as worthy and valuable. Each child has a unique mission and purpose that only he or she can accomplish in this world.

The following guidelines will help ensure that every child can thrive and grow up to become a worthy steward of our planet:

➢ Bring God in Your Child's Life

Children must be taught that they were put in this world for a purpose, and they were born with all the basic tools they need to accomplish this purpose. Adults must help children learn to make room for God in their lives, and to serve and trust Him. A parent does not need to be religious or even a *member* of any particular religion or faith to nurture love and awe of God. What children need are worthy role models.

These are the messages we need instil into our children:

- You are important to God.
- You are not here by accident.
- You have a unique mission to accomplish.
- God is constantly aware of you.
- God is always available to offer you guidance.

- You are accountable for all of your actions and choices.
- You possess all the qualities you need to fulfil your purpose.

➢ **Children Need Several Hours for Free Play Each Day**

All children need ample time for play, and a fair proportion of that time should be in the company of other children. The number and ages of playmates are not important. Even formal educational settings should actively support plenty of free playtime. Physical activity, including climbing and jumping, is essential for healthy development. It is sad that these activities are often regarded as dangerous in today's overprotective society.

Childhood is short. Free play is the single, most important element of childhood education. It is through unencumbered play that children learn to trust themselves, to negotiate, to think for themselves, to learn about their environments, and to thrive in social settings. Free play—with only minimal, peripheral supervision—provides children with the ideal forum for expressing ideas, honing their listening skills, problem-solving, sharing, cooperating, and assisting others. These are known as life skills.

- **Formal education should be secondary in importance to unencumbered play, open-ended, and autonomous.**

Formal education must be designed primarily to groom the future stewards of the universe. Giving children a clear message that they matter and that they are intrinsically valuable is infinitely more important than ensuring they possess thirteen years' worth of assorted, random, and arguably useless information.

Children who are introduced to a love of learning through challenging, fascinating and engaging material, and who have free access to a variety of sources of interesting information will read avidly on their own. They do not need to be bored silly by being spoon-fed material that they are quite capable of acquiring independently should they have the desire.

Of course, there is a place for some formal education as well. Children need to learn about the world they live in, and the different nationalities, religions, and cultures around the world. They would also benefit from exposure to mathematics, various the sciences, history, and geography, and as they grow older economics, government, and politics.

However, no formal learning should ever be at the expense of playtime—even for older children—quiet introspection time, or unencumbered reading time; and children should *never* be tested on what they have learned. Children also need to develop their muscles and hone their flexibility with plenty of physical activity. Sport, gymnastics, and swimming should be offered, but not enforced.

Rewards and punishments must be absolutely absent from a child's learning environment. Learning is about the child, not about the expectations of the adult trying to *teach* the child. More on this critical piece of information will follow in later chapters.

Lastly, children need ample time to develop their social, emotional and creative intelligences through social interaction with other children and liberal exposure to the arts and music. But most importantly, they need to know that they are worthy, they are indispensable, and they are ultimately accountable to themselves, to God, and to mankind.

I would like to point out that the above guidelines apply to all children up to around age *fourteen*, at which time most children will be beginning to show clear and definite preferences for the disciplines that truly speak to their innate natures.

➢ Children Need to Be Given Responsibility

They should be taught to help at home from a very early age. A one-year-old child can be taught to put toys away and help in other small ways. Older children can do almost anything an adult can do.

When they are rewarded with genuine appreciation, children love to help. Nothing else is needed to motivate children to take responsibility. Offering material or tangible rewards for taking responsibility is counterproductive and gives the wrong message.

Children should know from the outset that they are needed and expected to help out. Even small children can be taught to water the garden, make the beds, wash the dishes, and perform myriad other household chores. Sharing the workload at home allows children of all ages to see themselves as responsible, useful, and capable.

Children should also be given opportunities to help around their communities. They should be encouraged to do chores for elderly neighbours and friends, put away books at the local library, and create or join groups of children who meet for the purpose of cleaning up public areas such as the local beaches or parks.

- **Children should be involved in acts of goodness and kindness.**

Parents and teachers should regularly take children to hospitals and nursing homes to visit and cheer the people there. They can bring along handmade cards, treats, or toys. Children should be encouraged to befriend unpopular children by choosing them as playmates and inviting them to playdates and birthday parties. They should also be given the opportunity to personally give away outgrown clothing or toys to disadvantaged children in their neighbourhoods or nearby.

- **Children should be provided with ample exposure to nature.**

They should be given many opportunities to visit national parks, the seaside, farms, zoos, reserves, and other places of natural beauty. Camping trips are extremely beneficial to all children. All of these are among the many ways to develop love, appreciation, and understanding in a child's heart. These kinds of experiences serve to develop within children a deep appreciation of the world and its Creator and to want to protect it for future generations.

➢ National testing should be eliminated

So should external exams, competitions, and one-dimensional striving for top marks. All of these synthetic "benchmarks" have absolutely nothing to do with authentic education or preparation for adult life. Children are individuals. They have different strengths and talents, different natures and different gifts to share with the world. Schools should not be fixated on producing "high achievers." This practice greatly undermines the perceived value of every individual. Children are not the sum total of their academic abilities or their exam results!

It seems that formal, compulsory schooling has become nothing more than a babysitting service—an institution created to keep kids off the street and out of trouble. Filling children's heads with facts and figures for thirteen or more years of their young lives for the sole purpose of passing exams makes no sense! How much of what they learn in school do they really need to live happy, meaningful, and productive lives? What does a high score in final exams have to do with being a wise and thoughtful person, a contributing member of society, a worthy guardian, or an inspired, gifted leader? Nothing!

Instead, the entire school curriculum should be designed primarily to develop within each child essential qualities such as patience, thoughtfulness, compassion, humility, and gratitude. The only way to accomplish this is to ensure that the school employs only staff members and volunteers who model these character traits. Additionally, educators need to ensure that children develop a sense of responsibility to God and to mankind, a deep sense of appreciation for their own abilities and strengths, and for the gifts that their peers and mentors contribute to the school community.

Misconception Number 6

Children these days are expected to behave like little adults. When they don't, society believes there is something wrong with them.

The Facts

Children have a healthy need to **test** adult standards and practices. Children learn by *experimenting* and by *challenging*. They don't get life experience by following rules and directions. They learn about their world by playing it, experiencing it, and *challenging* what they learn and observe.

In today's society the testing and challenging that is normal childhood behaviour is thought to be unhealthy and is viewed with disapproval and fear. Adults do whatever they can to stop this natural process. Children quickly learn to be meek and/or compliant, or to suffer harsh consequences. Difficult children are shunned, punished, or medicated. (References: Caught in the Crossfire: Kids, Politics and America's Future; Kids: The Enemy within; The Diseasing of America's Children: Exposing the ADHD Factor: Redefining Childhood).

Misconception Number 7

Children who behave properly are well-adjusted and those who continually misbehave have "problems" that need to be "fixed."

The Facts

Children have two basic, **critical** needs after food, clothing, and shelter. They are **approval** and **relationship**. All children need deep, meaningful relationship, and all children need approval. They need these even more than they need love!

Unfortunately, most children end up having to **choose** between approval and relationship.

There are two basic kinds of children. Five out of every six children possess a core nature that motivates them to choose approval over relationship. These children are the fabric of society, the "good citizens." I call these children **head kids** because they naturally think about what they need to do to gain the approval—or at the very least avoid the disapproval—of the adults in their lives.

Conversely, one child in every six possesses a core nature that compels him or her to choose relationship over approval. I call these children **heart kids** because they don't *think* about what they are doing; they act on impulse. Their hearts motivate them to behave and function in ways that will get them the deep and meaningful relationships with adults that they desperately crave and need. (See ODD: A Guide for Families by the American Academy of Child and Adolescent Psychiatry; HRF Health Research Funding: 18 Intense Oppositional Defiance Disorder Statistics October 10, 2014.)

Heart kids possess an abundance of intensity, which is a gift given to them deliberately by God. They are fundamentally different from their peers. These "difficult children" are blessed with extra sensitivity, extra intelligence, and extra energy. They are not wired for compliance, nor are they wired to be "good citizens." They were born to be leaders—to *challenge* the status-quo—so society can continue to grow and develop.

Both kinds of children miss out on something critical to their healthy development: either approval or relationship! Misbehaviour is actually "***dis***-behaviour": a behaviour dysfunction caused by society's unwillingness to provide the deep connection and relationship children need without them having to resort to causing trouble.

Heart kids get lots of deep and meaningful relationship—loving correction, criticism, lectures, or punishments—but they don't get much approval at all! They are often ostracized with punishment, rejection, and medications. They attract frightening diagnoses, and they are taught to fear and hide their intensity. They learn at an early age not to trust their intuition, not to question, challenge, or test their environment. They are made to feel that there is something terribly wrong with them. The vast majority of children who end up with psychiatric diagnoses because of "behaviour challenges" are simply wired differently!

Head kids also suffer significantly, because they don't get nearly enough of the deep, meaningful connection and relationship that they really do need. They also learn to avoid questioning, challenging, and testing, believing that if they challenge, they are being "bad!"

Interestingly, many heart kids begin to flourish as they mature. They find themselves able to access and nurture the genius and creativity they never knew they possessed when they finally exit the education systems that had been suppressing and suffocating them throughout their childhoods. Conversely—and sadly—countless head kids are suffering from emotional illness or dysfunction and seeking professional help by the time they reach adulthood, because they have suddenly (or gradually) become aware that their whole lives have been played out not for themselves, but to satisfy the needs of the adults in their lives: their "good behaviour"—and even their academic "successes"—had been achieved largely to win approval!

Misconception Number 8

Good citizenship, moral standards, social skills, and values must be formally taught to children (and the best time to teach them is when a child makes a mistake or misbehaves).

The Facts

All children over the age of two know the difference between behaving and misbehaving, right and wrong, rule keeping and rule breaking; but heart kids end up making poor choices because they become addicted to the *highly charged relationship* they earn through negativity and problems, while the head kids are often left to seethe in resentment!

Infants are very busy during their first year of life. They spend most of their awake time observing their environments, and they draw most of their conclusions about life and society based on what they have observed. From about six months of age, they begin to discover that they get more intense and meaningful interactions from the adults in their lives when things start to go wrong.

A child of six months may bite her mother when she nurses, or throw his pacifier out of the crib, or his food from his high chair, just to get Mum or Dad's attention. A ten-month-old child will crawl toward the garbage bin, potted plant, or pantry—with the intention of emptying out its contents—simply to elicit a reaction from Mum or Dad.

By their second birthdays, many children have already established their own personas based on their keen observations. Very young children may come to see themselves as naughty, aggressive, needy, careless, or helpless, based on how adults react to their antics; and they may unconsciously play out these labels for years, or even for life!

Good citizenship is as natural as breathing to young children. It is only the interesting—and sometimes scary—reactions they get when they **mis**behave that confuse them. When adults learn the art of becoming animated in response to the *appropriate* choices children make instead of ignoring them, and at the same time they learn to "under-react" when children make poor choices, then children will default to appropriate behaviour and good citizenship.

Misconception Number 9

If we respond to broken rules with long, patient explanations, children will ultimately awaken to the wisdom of our words.

The Facts

The reason so many children keep engaging in behaviour that upsets us has *nothing* to do with them being unkind or naughty, not knowing it hurts or not knowing the rules. It has *everything* to do with relationship. Some children are simply captivated by the emotional connection they earn when they make poor choices. They become intrigued by the reactions they elicit when they find buttons to press or rules to break. We become their favourite toys! (This idea is explained and developed comprehensively in Howard Glasser's book *Transforming the Difficult Child,* a must-read for any parent or teacher.)

The first time a baby accidently bites his mother while nursing, he will "download" the mother's reaction of pain and shock. He will then remember this as a sure-fire way to gain the intense relationship with his mother that he craves. Small wonder some children will replay this fascinating "game," especially if the "offender" happens to be a heart child!

Bear in mind that there is not a shred of malice in the baby's mind when he revisits the bite-mum scenario: his motivation is fascination, not sadism! (This applies equally to very young children who hurt other children as well. They can't help but be fascinated by the chain of events they cause when they hurt someone. Unfortunately, such fascination often leads to unconscious self-labelling, which can last a lifetime!)

Many children respond to the *energy* rather than the content of what we tell them, because the need for relationship can easily eclipse a child's natural sense of justice. These children have simply concluded that the best way to get meaningful connection and relationship from adults is the best way to behave! Unfortunately, this happens more often when rules are being broken than when they are being kept.

Current thinking is that good citizenship, moral standards, social skills, and values must all be formally taught to children, and the ideal time to teach these life lessons is when something goes wrong. At such an opportunity, we are supposed to patiently and lovingly reprimand the culprits and attempt to help them see where they have erred. We are led to believe that if we are steadfastly loving and kind, and respond to broken rules with long, patient explanations, children will ultimately awaken to the wisdom of our words.

This does not bear out in practice. When we "lean in close" and lovingly tell children that they are not behaving appropriately or try in other ways to teach life lessons in response to broken rules, children absorb a much deeper truth: that we are much more *alive*, much more *available* to them, and much more *interested* in them when they make poor choices.

It seems to them that we adults just *love* when they make poor choices! They clearly see that they are more loved, more important, and more visible when things go wrong. The following truth is hard for a child to overlook: "I get handsomely paid with relationship and connection—when I'm being bad!"

Really it's only our *timing* that's wrong. Teaching rules, social skills, values, and life lessons when things go awry actually *causes* children to malfunction. Instead, we need to train ourselves to teach critical life lessons when they are being *demonstrated* by our children or students. The truth is that children are making wise choices at all times *except* when they are actually in the process of breaking a rule, so we have ample opportunity to shine the light on worthy values!

The next time your child makes a poor choice, try turning away from him or her for a few seconds. Reconnect when the negativity stops. Get animated when this child does the right thing and experience the wonder of "compliance by design!" Part 2 of this book will enlighten you with many exquisite tools or *healing agents* to help you "turn upside-down energy the right way up!" (a phrase coined by Howard Glasser, creator of The Nurtured Heart Approach).

Misconception Number 10

We need to be much tougher with children who are disruptive or oppositional.

The Facts

Children can develop an addiction to highly charged relationships. They can become so *intoxicated* by the energy you radiate at such times, that they end up playing **you** in the same way they play a computer game: they will play to win! As consequences and punishments (and energy) escalate, the child plays harder, because she is playing for higher stakes! Even when she protests loudly and extremely to consequences, she cannot back down, the highly charged atmosphere is too addictive. Attempting to appeal to a child's logic at a time like this is precisely like trying to reason with an alcoholic when he or she is way beyond rational thought.

Misconception Number 11

Children who cannot behave in acceptable ways need medications and therapy.

The Facts

What these children really need is a formula that works. You will find just such a formula in Part 2 of this book. Mind-altering medications act like a chemical prison. They do not heal; they simply mask the child's intensity until they wear off. Tragically, the administration of medications can impart a very scary message to a child: "There is something terribly wrong with me! My parents and teachers can't handle me, and my doctor can't help me!" This can leave a child frightened and desperate. A frightened, desperate child will fight back by acting out more extremely, and more often.

Medications

Medications are not always the only viable option for children with anxiety, depression, or conduct disorders. These can *all* be successfully treated in the vast majority of cases when the child's primary care-givers and teachers learn how to meet the child's core need for **approval** and **relationship** effectively. Having said that, a small percentage of such children may need or benefit from medical and/or psychological intervention—at least in the short-term—or until other therapies kick in.

Medications commonly prescribed for the out-of-control child can cause a host of worrisome side-effects such as stuttering, persistent blinking, nail-biting, appetite loss, chewing on clothing, sleep disorders, stomach trouble, anxiety, depression, dietary disorders, substance abuse, and occasionally life-threatening mental illness. Information about the dangers and harmful side effects of psychotropic medications is readily available.

Physicians, pediatricians, psychiatrists and psychologists would do well to educate themselves regarding more recent, less harmful, and equally (or more) effective interventions before writing out scripts or repeats. Besides the healing agents outlined in this book, folic acid and other nutrients have been found to be very effective treatments in some cases, particularly where gene mutations such as MTHFR and others are identified with simple blood tests.

Therapy

Therapy can be counterproductive or even addictive. Children have an underlying need for deep, meaningful, personal connection. Therapy is just another way for them to get this need met through negativity. They get to see this nice, kind, caring man or woman once a week/month/fortnight to talk about what? Their problems! They end up getting megadoses of failure messages *and* of relationship and "love", because of their problems! As much as they would *like* to improve and become more successful in life, these unfortunate children have become ensnared in the "therapy whirlpool."

Misconception Number 12

Rewards and punishments motivate children to behave better.

The Facts

Extrinsic punishments—and rewards—are harmful to children and unnecessary. Punishments usually end up becoming generous payment in the form of intense emotional connection and relationship for poor choices.

Rewards almost always end up being energy traps as well, as competition, jealousy, bargaining, pleading, cajoling, threats, and warnings usually revolve around them. The best way to motivate children to behave better is to create a system where the way they *feel* when they do the right (or wrong) thing is in itself the reward or otherwise. This is much better than behaviour management. This is transformation!

When children are rewarded for making wise choices with our interest and relationship and experience a *withdrawal* of our interest in them when they make poor choices, they are being given the gift of **clarity**. In part 2 of this book, you will learn some powerful ways to motivate and transform children by providing them with the clarity they need.

Children who experience the kind of clarity outlined in the following chapters are more than likely to become the fine human beings and stewards of the universe they were born to be. They will grow up to become upstanding citizens and leaders who are worthy, wise, eager, and well-prepared to dedicate themselves to a life of service to God, humanity, and the world; people automatically and amply blessed with happiness and fulfilment.

Summary

The Misconceptions

1. The world is doomed to destruction. Take what you can out of life!
2. Belief in God is unnecessary and maybe even harmful.
3. It is irresponsible to bring more children into the world as it is now.
4. You were born by accident or by chance.
5. The main purpose of childhood is to get the most comprehensive education possible.
6. There is something wrong with a child who doesn't listen or behave appropriately.
7. Anxious and oppositional children require medical and/or psychological intervention.
8. Moral standards, social skills, and worthy values must be formally taught to children, especially when they act inappropriately.
9. Eventually, children will awaken to the wisdom of our words.
10. We need to be much tougher with children who are disruptive and oppositional.
11. Children who cannot behave in acceptable ways need medications and therapy.
12. Rewards and punishments motivate children to behave better.

The Facts

1. God will never abandon us. We are part of the Divine plan.
2. Belief in God is essential, but religious bigotry can be devastating.
3. Children are God's gift to the world, our hope, and our salvation.
4. You were born by Divine design.
5. Childhood is the time to develop love for God, life, humanity, nature, and beauty.
6. Children who test and challenge authority figures are simply behaving like children.
7. All children require *relationship* and *approval* in order to function optimally.
8. Children don't need to be taught how to behave, they need to be recognised for the appropriate choices they make.
9. Children respond to the energy rather than the content of what we tell them.
10. Children will sometimes develop an addiction to highly charged relationships.
11. Medications and therapy are rarely necessary, and can cause untold harm.
12. Rewards and punishments are energy traps. Children need *clarity*.

Born to Serve

Creationist

I'm a creationist. If you are not, keep reading anyway. I'm not trying to convince you of anything. I'm just continuing my train of thought and bringing it to the next level. You may find some—or all—of what I am about to share quite interesting.

God seems to me to be the only truly feasible explanation for the incredible diversity, perplexity, precision, origin, purpose, and sheer magnificence of the universe. In fact, the only question belief in God doesn't answer is: God! If You truly exist, why do You hide Yourself so well? Why is life so *unfair*!

The catch is that belief in God imples a certain responsibility: it means that we are not free to do whatever we want if we owe our existence to a Higher Authority. We would have to consider the possibility that we are actually here for a purpose!

That said, we couldn't **believe** in God if it was **obvious** that He created life and personally scrutinized everything we did. God's existence would be an obvious fact, and we could not have the gift of free choice. We wouldn't be able to *choose* to enter into a relationship with our Creator. We could not even choose to rebel against Him!

We would be no different from any other creation, or from the angels. We would live our lives, fulfil our purposes, and die. There would be no concept of reward and punishment, and the world as we know it would not exist at all.

I see myself as God's handiwork, inserted into this world for a purpose that is unique to me. I am a tiny, insignificant, but indispensable piece of God's grand design. And insignificant as I am, my actions and choices are important to my Creator. I am both being held responsible for them against my will, and willingly taking responsibility for them.

To take this thought to the next level, I believe that God has given me a set of gifts, talents and experiences which inform the *kind* of service—to God, *and* to the world—He wants from me. My life experiences to date have been largely responsible for making me the person I am today. For just one simple example, if I didn't feel comfortable writing, I would not be writing this book!

Physical and Spiritual

Each of us has our own theory of evolution. I am going to briefly share the one I choose to buy into. It is the Torah version, clarified by the Kabbalah.

- There is One Supreme Being, who is the cause and the source of all else. He is alone and all of creation—physical and spiritual—is a part of Him. There is nothing in existence besides Him. He created everything—including time and space. We human beings can call Him whatever we wish—The Universe, Allah, God—it makes no difference. I will call Him God.
- Creation is not a momentous event which occurred long ago. Rather, every moment God *actively* brings everything into existence from the non-existence which preceded creation. When a human being creates something, only its form changes; the raw materials and the potential for creation were already there. Therefore, when the human disengages from the creative process, the object of his creation continues to exist independently. Conversely, God created the world *ex-nihilo*—from absolute nothingness and non-existence. Therefore, if G-d would

for one moment cease from actively bringing the universe into existence, it would instantly revert to the nothingness it came from.

- For reasons known only to Himself, God decided to become a Creator. He brought countless spiritual worlds into being, and one physical universe. He then chose to make this physical world—the "lowest" world of all—into His "home".
- God made the first human being in His own "image", calling him the *crown of creation*. He invested in us, and wants us to strive to become the best that we can be in order to help make our world into a place where He will want to "hang His hat."
- First, God created—and then followed—a code with which to create. This code is composed of ten stages, fiats, or utterances. In the Kabbalah they are referred to as the ten *sefirot*. They are the ten strand DNA, the building blocks of creation.
- Like any good architect, God began the creative process with a blueprint, which—according to tradition—is the Torah (Bible). God first created the Torah, then He looked into His Torah and created the world.

In His Form and Image

If God created our world in order to call it home and then charged humanity with the mission of transforming this home into a place where He will feel welcome and comfortable, He would have had to give us humans some direction. And He did. He gave us His precious blueprint—the Torah—to use as a road map. Every word, phrase, expression, and subtle variation or deviation in spelling or grammar in the Torah was dictated to His servant, Moses, with the express intention that we humans would be able to find hidden meaning and instruction. After all, the word Torah means instruction!

In Part 2 we will look at the creative process and how it can be used for personal and global healing, but let's jump ahead a little to the creation of man. God created man "in His form and in His image." What did God intend with these words? Many ideas have been expressed, but for now, let's go with this one: the capacity for intellectual and emotional expression. This means having the Godlike ability to think, feel, desire, speak, love, hate, pity, withhold, choose, and create. *We also have the ability to rebel and provoke.* Human ability goes beyond that of any other created being, *including angelic beings*, who do not possess free choice.

Good and Evil

God created a perfect world, and then He created Adam, the first human being, and placed him in the quintessential garden—the Garden of Eden.

Adam was also created perfect—male and female together in a single body—but when he saw that the animals all had mates, he wanted a companion of his own. So God separated the feminine qualities from the masculine ones and formed a woman from Adam's own flesh and blood. God then presented Eve (Chava—mother of all life) to him as his bride. So the perfect couple now inhabited the perfect garden in the perfect world. Things couldn't have been rosier.

For reasons known only to Himself, God was not happy with such a synthesized, balanced, and perfect world. He wanted some action. So God gave Adam just one commandment. Don't eat the fruit of the tree in the middle of the garden—a simple, totally doable request. Adam had absolutely no reason to object to a single, simple request from his Creator. But then God set the serpent loose in the garden.

The serpent's job was to tempt Adam. The cunning serpent approached Eve rather than try to directly cause Adam to rebel. Adam and Eve ate from the tree, and a counterbalance was introduced into the erstwhile perfect world: evil.

Now, evil is also a creation of God. As such, it is part of the Divine plan. When Adam and Eve sinned, they ingested a powerful urge to rebel against God. The force of evil is formidable, so God gave them an inclination for good as well—a thirst for God, for holiness, for the Divine, for goodness and kindness.

Our bodies house not one soul, but two. Our animal soul is concerned only for our material comforts and gratification. It does not desire nor recognise any Higher Authority. Our Godly soul is concerned only with the service of God. These two souls—or inclinations—are compared to two kings, constantly at war within us to gain control of the "small city", which is our choices and our actions.

If evil had a mission statement, it would sound like this: "There is none other but *me* to serve. What I want, I will have!" Conversely, good would have a mission statement as follows: "There is none other than **God alone**. I will serve Him faithfully with trembling and devotion—*with every fibre of my being*—all the days of my life."

Born to Serve

How does a human being serve God? After Adam was expelled from the Garden of Eden, God gave him a Code to adhere to, and to instruct his descendants to keep. Adherence to this Code *because it is the Will of God* is the key to world peace and harmony, eliciting God's protection and ensuring the world—along with all its inhabitants—endure and thrive. A person serves God by keeping His Laws.

The Code comprises seven Commandments, each with its own subset of do's and don't's. Violation of the Code constitutes rebellion against God, removes His overt loving protection, and exposes humanity to the threat of sickness, natural disasters, war, and strife. Keeping faithful to God's code means entering into a relationship with Him.

Human beings were born to serve. That is how God made us. We always have a choice. We can choose to serve ourselves, or to serve God. Service of God entails keeping this Code *for the sake of doing the will of God*. Service of ourselves means refusing to recognise our absolute dependence on God for our existence and the existence of the world and instead, behaving as we choose. Even if we would choose to adhere to the Seven Laws because they make sense to us, we would be serving ourselves (and our sense of reason) and not serving God.

The service of man is not like the service of an animal. All of creation is aware of its Creator and, simultaneously, of its own need to survive and procreate. The difference is that this awareness is natural and automatic for all life forms except man. Other life forms do not have the freedom to choose how they serve their Creator, nor how to use and modify their natural inclinations to survive. Their two inclinations are not in conflict. They are one.

Humans are different. Humankind is aware of its need to serve both its own physical requirements and its Creator. As these two needs are diametrically opposed to—and therefore in conflict with—each other, Adam's descendants found a way to "serve" a higher authority while still being able to indulge themselves. Their innovation was *idolatry*.

Worshipping (initially) the constellations allowed humanity to free themselves of the service of God, serve themselves instead, and delude themselves into believing that they were really serving God, by serving His ministering angels. It didn't take long before even this service was replaced by serving graven images which were supposed to be representations of godly powers.

Humanity soon forgot God entirely, and quickly descended into a state of total anarchy. God sent Noah to warn the world of impending disaster, going so far as to command him to spend *one hundred and twenty years* building an ark, just to motivate the populace to return to God and morality. The people ridiculed Noah, but miraculously were unable to harm, delay or deter him. Ultimately the world was destroyed and only Noah and his family were spared.

Seven Laws for Seventy Nations

After the flood, God made a pact with Noah and his descendants. He would not destroy the world again, but humanity must keep the Seven Laws He had originally given to Adam to protect society from endangering itself once more. God made a rainbow in the sky as a sign and a reminder for all generations that He is present, and that He expects humans to rise above their self-serving and destructive tendencies. As these laws were now entrusted to Noah and his family, they became known as The Seven Noahide Laws, or **The Noahide Code**.

Over the next few generations, the Noahide Code was again abandoned. At Mount Sinai God commanded Moses to instruct the newly formed Jewish nation to teach the Noahide Code to the seventy nations of world. This commandment is one of the 613 Commandments given to the Jews.

These are the laws God gave to mankind through Adam, Noah and finally, Moses:

1. To believe in God
2. Not to rebel against Him, nor worship idols
3. Not to murder
4. Not to commit adultery
5. Not to steal anything for any reason
6. Not to tear a limb from a living creature
7. To establish courts to enforce these laws

God's purpose in creating man was to bring His Divine plan to fruition. Our job description: to make room for God in our lives—on *His* terms, by adhering to the Noahide Code. This is far from easy, because our animal and Divine souls are constantly at war with each other to control our behaviour.

Global adherence to the Noahide Code—with the intention to do the will of God and **not** because they appeal to our sense of reason—will cause evil to be banished from the world forever, will allow man's two opposing poles of service to be brought into sync, and will enable God to finally feel at home.

Man versus God

In today's upside-down world, we are led to believe that morality is arbitrary, and that feeding our natural tendencies is essential for our mental health and happiness. Both of these beliefs are categorically untrue. Indulging in practices which are explicitly forbidden is outright dangerous. Our only hope for healing and happiness is the full embrace of God and the Noahide Code. We must learn to *curb* our desires, passions, and tendencies, not indulge them!

Those who are most vocal in the *human rights movement* are deliberately leading the vulnerable people among us astray, and making it illegal for us to stop these poor souls from causing further harm to themselves and to the world. Human beings don't have rights, they have responsibilities: to themselves, to God, to humanity, and to the world.

Human rights activists are trying to destroy and demolish any hope of a stable and safe society by having legislation passed which puts the young, the humiliated, the helpless, and the vulnerable at extreme, life-threatening risk. To make it absolutely clear that they are at war with God, and to spitefully add insult to injury, these protagonists of evil and immorality have chosen the rainbow as their banner!

It's Under Control

This world is in dire straits. If God wanted to wipe us out again, He wouldn't have to bring another flood. He wouldn't have to do anything at all but wait a little, because we are headed for self-destruction fast! Just look at how governments around the world—which are supposed to be there to protect us—are **wooing and funding** evil and destruction! But we don't need to worry, because God has not abandoned us. He is waiting for us just beyond the wall of our own limitations, "peeking through the cracks" in the words of the Lubavitcher Rebbe. He is there, guiding us, trusting us, supporting us, and encouraging us.

All we need to do is recommit ourselves to serving Him. We can also choose to take our commitment further and cultivate **love** and **awe** of God! We can do this through the focused study of His Code, by spending our free time looking for opportunities to do random acts of goodness and kindness, and by looking for God's "fingerprints"—clues He constantly leaves for us—to help us to rediscover His presence in this world and His very personal interest in us. We tend to call His clues coincidence or serendipity, but they are actually His call to us to look for Him, find Him, and welcome Him into our lives.

Why did God go to such lengths to hide from us and then reach out to us in such a "circumnavigational" way? Out of kindness. He wanted to invite us humans to *willingly* become partners in Creation by establishing a home for Him on Earth, and to set the foundation for global healing. To help us along, God gave us children. **Our children are the stewards of the universe.** Children know God. They are the key to the survival of our planet and the universe, and to the fulfilment of God's Divine plan. That's why the way we raise and educate our children is so important.

Adam Kadmon

Let's take another look at the creation of Adam, the first man. Adam was created in God's image. First, God created a prototype of the human being. This spiritual prototype is called "Adam Kadmon," the supernal man, a reflection of God. What you are about to learn is figurative, as God has no physical form. Adam Kadmon is simply a representation of the Divine qualities, which are reflected in the human body and soul. Having said that, I am now going to draw a picture of him.

There are two powerful forces that act upon and fundamentally affect the human being and the faculties of our souls. They are **delight** and **will**. Delight and will sit above the brains in Adam Kadmon's head. They are like a crown, or like hair, that encompass the brain, and they are profoundly influential. Both desire and will are above reason. They are *encompassing* soul powers, and they unobtrusively inform every choice we make.

Adam Kadmon's head represents intellect, the source of reason. Reason is divided into the subfaculties of *chachmah, bina,* and *da'at*—wisdom, understanding, and knowledge.

Adam Kadmon has a right side and a left side. The right side is the side of love; the left side is the side of fear. Respectively, they bring close and repel. Together, they create the tension that is the rhythm of life. Love is inhalation, acceptance. Fear is exhalation, rejection.

Both are spawned by either delight or will (or both), and both are manifest in all of our decisions. The pumping of the heart also reflects their influence, simultaneously pumping oxygen into the blood and pumping out toxins. Love and fear themselves are the "arms," or "wings," of Adam Kadmon. *The right arm embraces, while the left arm repels.*

After the initial triggers of delight or will, love and fear affect and inform our reasoning, and ultimately our actions.

Love—the right hemisphere—is the source of embracing an idea (in the brain), and the traits of love, trust, kindness, acceptance, and excitement and their offshoots (in the heart).

Fear—the left hemisphere—is the source of challenging an idea (in the brain), and the traits of fear, severity, rejection, anger, and boundaries and their offshoots (in the heart).

The **heart** (midpoint) of Adam Kadmon is the actual source of love and fear, kindness and severity, acceptance and rejection. From the right side of the heart comes the ability to see what's acceptable and desirable; from the left side of the heart comes the ability to set limits and boundaries. In the heart centre they combine to create a space to move forward: **compassion** and **forgiveness**.

The **kidneys** of Adam Kadmon are the source of the rest of the human set of emotions, which are all derivatives love, fear, and compassion. The **reproductive organs** are the birthing of action resulting from the work of the kidneys, which break down and assimilate the processes of the brain and heart. The **legs** carry out the actions that have been birthed.

This is a very brief synopsis of how the human body and soul is a reflection of the Divine, and how our will, delight, reasoning, and emotions inform our actions and the way we behave and respond to stimuli. All of this information will become clearer and more meaningful as you progress through this book.

Qualities in Negative

The quintessential manifestations of love and fear are the soul's burning passion and desire to perform the will of God, and its dread and terror of opposing God's will. The reason that these qualities have become so muddied is because of the evil planted within us. These qualities are tempered and dampened almost to the point of extinction by the human being's *self*-love and *self*-preoccupation.

As mentioned, our bodies house two souls: our Divine soul (good inclination) that desires only to do the will of God; and our animal soul (evil inclination), whose only desire is **self**-gratification. Our job is to nurture the tiny sparks of love and fear of God that are found in our Godly souls, and fan them into raging fires of passion for God.

This is accomplished by taking our brute passion for our own needs, wants, and desires, and using it as jet fuel for fulfilling God's will, by ***not*** indulging them when they conflict with His will.

Once you set your heart and mind firmly on accomplishing this, you will find God right by your side, aiding and assisting you so that you will succeed. Avoth 2:4 gives us this advice: "Make His will your will and He will make your will His will. Nullify your will before His will, and He will nullify the will of others before your will."

Just before I get to the actual process of creation and healing, I will clarify my reasoning for introducing you to the Torah's account of creation, the Kabbalistic doctrine of the purpose of creation, and man's Divine mission. Each human being is a microcosm of the entire universe. Just as each of our Godly souls reflect the Divine attributes, our evil inclinations—or animal souls—reflect the exact opposite: those very qualities in negative.

We have Divine attributes, and we have animalistic drives, which are nothing but Divine attributes gone *wrong*. Our job is to rectify these attributes and realign them to their purpose: to be used in the service of God.

Now we can begin to understand the point of having, raising, and educating children. We were put into an imperfect world and given the mission to perfect it. We are incredibly challenged because we can barely tell the difference ourselves between right and wrong. Our animal soul is persistent, loud, demanding, and convincing. Our Divine soul can barely be heard above the din. God has hidden Himself very well in this world so that we must search diligently to find Him. We have plenty to deal with.

Then we are faced with children. Children are a reflection of the best and the worst in us. We revel in the good that they bring into the world and our lives: the love, fun, freshness, wonder, innocence. And then we are completely thrown and bewildered by the rest of what they throw at us.

This is where the energy connection comes in. Children need our relationship so badly that they easily learn the best ways to get it. We are meant to see through the game and perceive the point of it all, which is to heal and perfect ourselves, our families, and ultimately, the world! What drives us crazy in kids (and difficult adults) is a reflection of what we need to fix in ourselves. By mastering the way we respond—**not react**—to broken rules and negativity, we learn to master our own natures.

In this sense, the child is like the evil inclination, challenging us with his or her banner:

"There is nothing other than *me* to serve. *You* shall serve *me* by giving me the deep, meaningful emotional connection I desire and need, at all costs!"

Your response should be to take the role of the good inclination and carry this banner: "There is nothing other than God to serve! I will provide you with *your* needs in response to *you* learning how to make your will *His* will. **We are in this together.** It's no longer *me* against *you*; it's *we* becoming a team, and *together* healing, taming, and transforming ourselves, each other and the world!" In Part 2 of this book, you will learn exactly how to do that.

You have now graduated Part 1. Welcome to Part 2—Building Blocks!

PART 2

BUILDING BLOCKS

A Guide for All of Humanity

BUILDING BLOCKS

Seven stones build 5,040 houses,
And ten utterances build the entire universe.

In 2009 I read *Transforming the Difficult Child* by renowned psychotherapist Howard Glasser. I had been working with children for more than three decades before I read this book, and was still unable to figure out why some children (and adults!) **self-sabotage** over and over again! I was taken by the way Glasser masterfully explained the connection between misbehaviour and relationship.

In this book (and his subsequent books), Glasser guides his readers through an innovative emotional healing programme called The Nurtured Heart Approach. Through extensive research and experimentation, Glasser discovered the healing agents outlined in the following pages and coined fitting names for them. He then lovingly supplied analogies, associations, stories, and terminology to assist with understanding and implementation. By

Divine providence, his approach is stunningly reflective of the ten **sefirot**—building blocks—of Creation. I humbly thank you, Howard, for sharing your invaluable tools with me and with all of humankind, and for dedicating your every breath to benefit humanity.

Building Blocks

The ten **sefirot** are the building blocks of creation, and of healing. They have names that describe their functions. Roughly translated they are *chachmah*—wisdom, *bina*—understanding, *da'at*—knowledge, *chesed*—kindness, *gevurah*—restraint, *tiferet*—beauty, *netzach*—victory, *hod*—splendour, *yesod*—foundation, and *malchut*—sovereignty.

Chachmah, bina, and *da'at* are our thought processes; *chesed, gevurah, tiferet, netzach, hod,* and *yesod* are our emotions; and *malchut* is action. Above and beyond them all are *ratzon* and *chefetz*, will and desire (delight). God desired a home in a lowly, physical universe, and willed it to come into being. Then He employed the ten sefirot as the building blocks to execute His plan. These sefirot can be used as the basis of any creative process:

Chachmah is the seminal idea, the flash of inspiration.

Bina is all the details that bring form and substance to the idea.

Da'at is the organization of information to plan the creative process.

Chesed is the free generation of inspiration.

Gevurah is the creation of boundaries and parameters, and the editing process.

Tiferet is the arrangement of all the data into a viable product.

Netzach is the form the final product takes.

Hod is the finishing touches.

Yesod is the soul—bringing the creation to life.

Malchut is the practical application, the completion, the finished product in action.

Sechel and *Middot*

Chachmah, bina, and da'at involve the ***sechel***, the cognitive faculties of your soul. The next six sefirot involve the ***middot***, the emotional faculties. The last *sefirah* is malchut, action—the actual healing process. If you have the desire and the will to use the sefirot to heal, you need to first employ your sechel and then your middot.

The first phase of your healing journey will be the sechel phase. Chachmah is identifying the problem. Bina is understanding the ramifications of the problem. Da'at is creating a game plan to resolve the problem. Welcome to the sechel phase of your journey!

Chachmah—Wisdom

Chachmah is the first sefirah. It derives from the "right," the side of love. Chachmah is the essence of understanding. It is the seminal idea—the *aha* moment, the sensation of a flash of lightning when something fundamental and astounding is about to be discovered.

My own aha moment occurred when I discovered the connection between misbehaviour and meaningful relationship. Misbehaviour *does* elicit satisfying emotional connection. The juicy reward of a highly charged emotional reaction to provocation is compelling.

Summary: Chachmah = "We make poor choices because it pays."

Bina—Understanding

Bina is the second sefirah. It derives from the "left," the side of fear. Bina is the *restraint* of the free flow of energy. Bina is understanding. It is a process. It is the collection of information and thoughts that give the initial flash of inspiration shape and form, meaning and depth. Bina is the process of making sense of the correlation between behaviour and relationship.

Fundamental to successful parenting and teaching is understanding the intrinsic connection between the choices children make and how we respond to and influence those choices. When we make the conscious decision to interact with children as "creators" rather than "reactors," we can transform their motivation to repeat or to alter their behaviour, as well as their perception of who they are.

Summary: Bina = "How I initiate interaction and respond to provocation determines whether I harm or heal."

Da'at—Knowledge

Da'at is the third sefirah. It derives from the "centre," the seat of compassion and beauty. It is the ability to moderate the free flow of energy. Da'at is the ability to form conclusions and develop strategies based on what we have learned.

Once we understand the connection between provocation and reaction—as well as the motives that draw people into this "dance"—we can use reason and *healing agents* to modify the sequence of events and ultimately change the dance.

Summary: Da'at = "I can transform people by modifying my use of energy."

Global Healing

Many children discover very early in their lives that problems and misbehaviour win them *the gift of intimacy* with at least one important adult, and often more than one. Subsequently, they find out that more negativity, more problems, or more opposition and defiance lead to **deeper and more profound connection** and relationship with these adults, and sometimes with a team of professionals as well. By this time, these children are trapped, and their parents and teachers are pulling their hair out. They have become literally **addicted** to negativity or problems (or both). Tragically, they then become quite convinced that they are just bad, sick, or stupid! Here is an illustration of how a parent's well-meaning words can actually cause harm:

Imagine that you have a seven-year-old son called Johnny who is avoided by his classmates. He is aggressive, angry and noncompliant. It seems that he was just born with a difficult and aggressive nature. Now if you knew that eighteen-month-old Johnny would become a bully based on how his immature mind processed well-meaning instructions, you would most likely change the language you used in order to provide him with the clarity and feedback he needed.

If only you had known, you would have said, "Johnny, I see that you are being very gentle with your little brother" *before* he started getting rough, instead of saying, "Now be gentle, Johnny!" *after* the event.

You would have said, "I just noticed you waiting patiently for your chance to play with that," before he grabbed, instead of saying, "No grabbing, Johnny!" after the event!

What you didn't know was that very young children tend to take us very literally. If Johnny is a bully now, it is likely that at some point in his first or second year of life, he **labelled** himself a bully, based on information he collected and interpreted.

In both the above scenarios, Johnny might have said to himself, "I'm not a good person. I am rough. I have no patience. I'm not nice." These assumptions could easily have caused Johnny to **label** himself aggressive and adopt that persona without ever challenging it!

You might have even accidently *encouraged* him to become a bully by providing him with inadequate connection and relationship (*intimacy*) when he was not doing anything wrong, but suddenly becoming **alive** and **very** interested in him when he was misbehaving or threatening to misbehave. This could easily have caused Johnny to come to the unconscious conclusion that he is more interesting, esteemed, and even more **loved** when he is aggressive.

Here is another illustration:

Imagine you have a nine-year-old daughter called Samantha. Sam suffers from anxiety, poor self-esteem, assorted learning challenges, and poor concentration. She is disorganized and gets overwhelmed easily. Now if you had known when she was a year old that Sam was predisposed to becoming insecure and dependent, you might have handled things differently.

If only you had known, you would have said, "Sam, I see that you are really focused on your drawing," *before* she started getting frustrated, instead of saying, "Come on, Sam—you can do it!" too late!

You would have said, "Look how well you are managing that without any help!" before she dissolved into tears, instead of saying, "Let me help you with that," after the event!

If Sam is not coping without significant support now, it is likely that at some point in her very early childhood, she **labelled** herself incompetent and unable to deal with stress, based on information she collected and incorrectly interpreted.

It is likely that Samantha, in her first two years of her life, had too many opportunities to come to the conclusion that she can't manage on her own and needs help from an adult. You might have even accidently encouraged this by becoming very interested and **alive** when Sam was struggling with some activity, task, or emotion, and possibly jumping in to advise or help too soon. Sam may have even concluded that she matters more when she isn't coping! She probably labelled herself helpless long before she had the ability to think rationally and make an accurate assessment of her ability.

The same sequence of cause and effect, labelling and disabling, that affects children so fundamentally may adversely affect adults as well. If the labels we carry were formed and "downloaded" before we could think logically, we may have grown up accepting them as a part of who we are, never imagining that we can challenge and discard them.

In the early, critical stages of our own development, our proclivity to go for the gold when it came to a chance at deep, meaningful relationship may have led many of us down the road of poor choices in life, self-sabotage, emotional dysfunction, addiction, or a combination of these and other harmful behaviour patterns. The root cause of all of these curses was—and still is—our compelling attraction to **emotional energy,** or, put differently, our need for *intimacy*. Maybe even as a species, this has been the story of our lives!

How does this relate to global healing? The "evil" in the world is the need for us humans to have our own needs met before the needs of others, and sometimes even at the expense of others' needs. It's the **give-me-it's-mine!** phenomenon. People—including adults—need meaningful relationship and will sometimes resort to misbehaving, breaking rules, or hurting others in order to get their relationship needs met.

We all know God. We call on Him when the going gets tough. And we blame Him when things go wrong. We do this even if we don't believe in Him. We say things like, "God if You really existed You wouldn't let this happen!" Just like spoiled children, we forget Him when life is good, and we reject Him when things don't go our way. If we could connect with Him in a meaningful way *before* things began to turn sour, we might be able to enjoy some meaningful and desirable intimacy with Him!

Is it possible that throughout history, man has misbehaved and rebelled against his Creator, at least subconsciously, in order to elicit a reaction from Him? Would we humans rather be the recipients of God's wrath than His seeming disinterest in us? If we look at the course of history, we can see a pattern, and it goes like this: provocation, punishment, provocation, punishment! **What would happen if we chose to *serve* instead of provoke?** To put our own needs aside, and selflessly serve God? How might He respond?

I posit that humanity is suffering from an **energy disorder** which could technically be fitted with a diagnostic appellation such as *Disbehaviour* Syndrome, or DS. Every day untold damage is being done by influential and powerful people with DS! The river of damage will continue to flow until we acquire enough evidence of our innate goodness to abandon our self-inflicted labels in favour of labels that accurately reflect who we really are!

In truth, every single one of us was created in God's image, with everything we need to lead wholesome, happy, worthy, wealthy, and purposeful lives. We need a practical, effective way to get back in touch with our inner selves and with our Father and Creator. He is waiting for us to return to Him, to return to our true selves.

If you want to test this thought, you can try this simple experiment: every day for a week begin each day—the moment you open your eyes—with the following prayer: "Thank you, living and eternal King, for restoring my soul to me today! Thanks for showing Your faith in me! In appreciation, I am going to do something for **You** today!" Keep your commitment by doing something nice for a family member, friend, or colleague once or repeatedly through the day. Look out for the Divine response you might experience from such provocation!

At the end of the week, assess the impact of your commitment. If you like the way you feel and you are game to continue experimenting, you can take this idea further. Make a habit of performing acts and gestures of goodness and kindness to random people on a regular basis. Set a goal of ten or twenty unsolicited kind gestures a day.

If you really love somebody, you love his or her children as well. We are all God's children. God gave each one of us the gift of **life**. One way to show our gratitude to God is to give the gift of kindness to someone else (another child of God). Go ahead. Do a random act of goodness and kindness by validating someone in a meaningful way!

True Power

Your soul has ten powers and three garments. The soul's garments reveal its powers. The powers of the soul are the sefirot, which we have already discussed. Its garments are thought, speech, and action. Thought reveals your sechel, your reason. Speech reveals your middot, your emotions. Action reveals malchut, your level of self-mastery.

God used ten utterances in the creative process. Each utterance began with the word *yehi*—let there be. God employed the ten sefirot in the creation of the world. Each of the ten sefirot relates to one of the ten utterances. Interestingly, God used the power of *speech* to create the world. God conceived the idea of a world (chachmah), planned the details (bina), designed a blueprint—the Torah (da'at), and followed through with active creation (the next six sefirot). He introduced a new sefirah for each of the six days of Creation.

God rested on the seventh day but constantly continues to actively animate the universe (malchut). Without God's active and constant creative force—which is God's speech—the world and all existence would automatically revert to the nonexistence it came from.

Speech is a faculty and gift God gave to humans exclusively. Human beings were made to be creators. Just like God, when we speak, things **happen**. What we say and how we say it has incredible power. In fact, speech is the most potent creative agent we possess. Thoughtless or malevolent speech can destroy a person, or even—theoretically—the world! Wisely chosen words can save, reform, or transform a person and the universe.

Mastering your speech ultimately comes down to mastering your heart and your mind.

You have now become the creator of your own healing journey. You have just employed chachmah, bina, and da'at—your sechel—in completing the first phase of your journey. Now you are going to learn how to apply the next six sefirot—your middot—to set in motion some very precise remedial procedures designed to reach, awaken, and heal yourself and others.

You will learn how to **respond** instead of to react. You will no longer *teach* appropriate behaviour, good manners, and values, but enable all the **switches** that have been disabled over time. You are now ready to learn how to free the people who matter to you to return to their default settings of ability, goodness, wisdom, and self-control. And you will learn how to do the same for yourself.

The true definition of power is the ability to control your impulses and emotions. As you are now aware, the key to transformation is to turn **upside-down energy** the right way up. Not exploding when you feel the need is the ultimate show of power and strength. Notching up your energy levels when things are going **right** is the ultimate way to teach and to heal. All of these skills involve the power of speech.

You have already begun your healing journey. Until this point, you have been immersed in the intellectual-cognitive stages of the creative process. You have identified the problem, analysed the different facets of it, been introduced to the history and ramifications of your aha moment, and come to see the problem in a much clearer, lucid, concrete way. You **know** what's wrong and why. The next part of your journey is the speech part; it's about harnessing your emotions and using their power as jet fuel for transformation.

Welcome to the middot phase of your journey!

Chesed—Kindness

Chesed is the fourth sefirah and the first healing agent. It derives from the "right," the side of love. Chesed is the free flow of kindness. The Torah begins with the words, "In the Beginning, God created the heavens and the Earth. The Earth was desolate and void, and covered in darkness. God said Let there be Light, and there was light."

God created the world with kindness. The creative process began and continued until completion with a surge of chesed, kindness. This is obvious from the fact that the creations that came into being didn't do anything to deserve to be created—they were just gifted with life! Before any other creative activity could happen, light was provided. Nothing will grow without light. Light is chesed, kindness.

Chesed is the first and most important healing agent. It is the "**ICU**" of healing. The intensive care unit is where a casualty is stabilized in preparation for further treatment. Chesed is the healing agent that prepares the "casualty" (you and me, and the rest of humanity) for further healing.

Chesed is the gift of acceptance. It is administered by flooding your home or workplace with pure kindness by frequently using carefully worded statements designed to *validate the existence* of the people you spend your time with.

Chesed is the critical foundation that all of the following healing agents are built on. It is astoundingly easy to administer: simply **initiate** relationship using the words "**I see you.**" Do this frequently, dozens of times a day. That's all there is to it!

Here are some good examples of the kinds of things you might say:

- Donald, I see you working on that problem. You're concentrating hard and not giving up.
- Monica, I see that you have finished your sandwich. Would you like another one?
- David, I see you playing that game with such determination! You are totally focused!
- Tom, I notice that you have decided to finish your homework later on. It looks like you were getting pretty frustrated and decided you needed a break.
- Tony, I just saw you walking away from Amanda. You made the choice not to argue with her.
- Linda, I see that you are taking your three favourite dolls with you. You have bundled them all into your baby sling!
- Mum, I see that you finished the book you were reading yesterday and have begun a new one!

I have provided you with quite a substantial list of examples of how you might employ this first step toward healing. Here's why. I wanted to clearly demonstrate the following:

- ✓ You are simply validating the person's existence. You can do this for anyone of any age.
- ✓ You are reflecting back what you see, keeping it really simple.
- ✓ You are deliberately steering clear of giving an opinion. It's not about you.
- ✓ You are not giving advice or lecturing.
- ✓ You are not adding value statements. At this stage, they could sound patronizing.
- ✓ You are speaking from your heart. Your sole intention is to connect meaningfully with the person you are addressing.
- ✓ It's quick and easy enough to administer several times a day to any number of people.
- ✓ It's sincere and honest, and it's not hard to do!

"I see you" is the "**ICU**" of healing. It's an astoundingly therapeutic way to engage meaningfully with the people you work with or care for. Don't ever use this intervention to admonish or challenge. Its sole purpose is to see and validate people. Therefore, it is essential that you use it only *when nothing is going wrong!* You may need to build up a tolerance for speaking in this way because it might sound a little odd or weird to you to begin with.

Chesed is a very powerful healing agent. With this first emotional nutrient, you begin to condition yourself and others to hear (and speak) in ways that are not judgmental! We all have the wisdom to do the right thing. What we are lacking is the right environment and a healthy belief in our own innate goodness. Chesed is the first essential step in changing that.

Difficult children often don't really fit in socially. Their friends (if they have any) share with them very little besides the desperate need to create meaningful relationships with the significant adults in their lives. They band together because they feel that they have been born on the wrong planet! They struggle with feelings of inadequacy and feel the need to justify their right to exist. They wonder whether they have any purpose or contribution to make.

Difficult adults also have a much greater need to be seen, noticed, validated, and energized than their contemporaries. When we make the choice to interact with them on our own terms, we don't have to wait for them to be difficult, contrary, needy, or oppositional. We simply make sure to notice them and engage with them meaningfully when nothing is going wrong!

That's right. The best way to connect with a person in a meaningful way is to engage with him when nothing's going wrong! Using the words "I see you," reflect back what you see at regular intervals. It works like drip-irrigation on parched soil. It tells the recipient

- You are on the right planet!
- You have a right to exist!
- You are here for a purpose!

It is the most effective way to let people know that they matter!

The recipient has not done anything to warrant your attention and has not in any way *earned* your relationship. You have simply shown up randomly and given her a free gift of your energy. And you have not moderated or adulterated that gift with your thoughts, opinions, suggestions, advice, approval, or expectations. This is pure chesed—a gift.

To ensure this healing agent achieves its purpose be careful to do the following:

➢ Don't use this to reflect behaviour you don't want the recipient to engage in or repeat.

- Don’t ever speak when you are distraught or angry. Wait for the negative feelings to pass.
- Don’t force it. Conceive the statement in your head, but then say it with your heart.
- Begin by practicing on yourself, a partner or friend who knows that you are practicing, or when talking to small children to give you the opportunity to get used to the sound of it.
- Begin with just a few a day with older children or adults, but increase the frequency, intensity, and duration of your reflections very quickly.
- Use it to validate everyone you interact with, not just oppositional or difficult people.
- Speak sincerely and convincingly.

I want to make the following crucial point. If you don’t want all of your study and efforts to backfire, I advise you to take this very seriously: Don’t ever validate one person with the hope that someone else not doing the right thing will be motivated to follow suit; or even worse, to make a point that the other party is not doing the right thing. If used in this way it is not validation at all, it’s *manipulation!*

You are abusing the whole healing programme just to satisfy your own need for compliance or cooperation! Both the intended recipient and anyone else who hears you will be very put off if you try to use such tactics to try to force compliance. This will cause anger and resentment, and may make it much harder for others to take you seriously when you later make genuine efforts to validate them.

Here's another related and very important point: Begin each statement with the person's name, and use the word ***you***, as in, "Daniel, I see you …" If you say, "I see Daniel …" you sound like a sports commentator. You are not speaking to the intended recipient at all! This will also sound very much like manipulation to anyone who hears you, even if your intention was sincere.

This first healing agent is quite simple to implement, but astoundingly therapeutic. Even if you find it somewhat awkward at first, you will quickly come to appreciate its incredible healing power. *Initiating* meaningful relationship at frequent intervals as prescribed will enable **you** to begin to take control of your own emotions and **others** to begin to see themselves as worthy. It's a win-win. This is the "**ICU**" of healing.

Summary: Chesed = "I see you!"

Gevurah—Boundaries

Gevurah is the fifth sefirah and the second healing agent. It derives from the "left," the side of fear. It is the restraint and control of the free flow of kindness. "On the second day God created a **firmament** to separate the waters above from the waters below."

Water is another metaphor for kindness, but abundant water that is not contained or channelled effectively can be devastating! The word *gevurah* has many meanings: strictness, severity, justice, restraint, boundaries, strength, power, limits. They all imply restriction.

Gevurah is the gift of boundaries. From the second day of Creation, the heavenly spheres and the material universe were each provided with boundaries and limits. Chesed is like a blank check, which is **worthless** (and potentially ruinous) until a withdrawal amount is filled in. The amount written on the check is the boundary that makes it useful. The account may contain millions of dollars, but absolutely nothing can be withdrawn with a blank check. The dollar amount is gevurah. It defines the worth of the check.

Chesed and gevurah can now be understood in terms of "lights and vessels." Light is unlimited; vessels limit the light and contain it. If the light was not contained, it would be of no benefit at all. Kindness without boundaries would soon create chaos. Chesed is the free flow of relationship, and gevurah is the withdrawal of relationship. The interplay of chesed and gevurah creates a "dance."

Now it's time to learn the dance. Here are the steps: Address random people using the words "I see you" as often as you can, ideally every ten minutes or less. Start to make your statements longer, more meaningful, and more heartfelt as your skill grows.

Ensure everyone you interact with is verbally acknowledged (validated) several times a day, especially the more challenging (heart) people, while at the same time making sure not forget the more easy-going (head) people. Keep this up **as long as no negativity is happening.**

Now is the time to *expect* adversity. Don't fear it. It *needs* to make an appearance sometime soon. This will be your opportunity to make a stand. At this point, you are creating the framework for the boundaries that make this healing programme *work.*

When the adversity arrives, be ready for it. Immediately **disconnect** all relationship with the "offender", without saying why. Do this by casually turning your back on the person. Slowly count to ten while breathing into the centre of your heart. Feel and accept your feelings, whatever they are. Allow them to peak and subside. Don't let the offender see any evidence of fear, frustration, anger, or hurt.

Congratulations! You have just executed your very first real show of gevurah! You have just **refused to energize** the negativity that was thrown at you. You took a genuine stand; enjoy the experience! You are employing *determination* to become a master at controlling your impulses. The determination *not* to react is gevurah.

Now reconnect and pick up where you left off. Don't show any trace of lingering bad feelings. Don't *ever* mention the incident that just happened. **Let it go**. If you don't let it go, you are energizing it in retrospect, which is counterproductive. To be able to do this, it will be necessary for you to swallow your pride. It is natural to feel a sense of indignation when your expectations are not met, but it's well worth the sacrifice. You are learning to play a new game—the game of healing!

If you ask someone to do something and he refuses, procrastinates, or ignores you, let it go. The same applies to any other negativity. When someone is disrespectful, mean, or rude, let it go. Resist the urge to correct, nag, punish, warn, lecture, cajole, admonish, or otherwise try to force compliance.

What *should* you do? Turn away for a few seconds. *That's it!* If you want to create healing, you have to trust that people will learn to self-correct and self-manage within a very short time—**if** you use these healing agents exactly as prescribed.

Imagine you are in a high-school classroom, having a lively discussion with a group of teenagers. You are fully attentive and available for the free flow of energy and relationship with everyone in the room as long as no one says or does anything undesirable or hurtful (to you, or to anyone else). The moment someone does, you instantly go offline by turning away *from that individual only* for a few seconds.

Behave as if that person has just tripped the wire that connects her to your source of energy! Of course, you remain online for everyone else in the room. As soon as the negativity or rule breaking stops, you re-establish the connection with no residual effect.

The offender will quickly discover that she has the power and ability to stay online with you by keeping within the boundary lines. When she errs and says or does something inappropriate and you immediately disconnect in response, she knows that she can count on you to quickly re-establish connection with her and that you will not hold her slip against her or embarrass her in front of her friends.

By moderating chesed with gevurah in this manner, you enable your free flow of kindness to be immeasurably more powerful and effective. And that makes *you* much more powerful and effective as well! Like your Creator, you have created lights and vessels.

Chesed and gevurah are the most difficult healing agents to master, because they differ so radically from common practice. When someone's behaviour is wanting, people naturally want to put all of their energy into trying to "fix" that person and *solve* his or her problems.

When the focus is on problem solving and external control and correction, the owner of the problem is a *failure* in his own estimation. When the focus is on creating the right environment for self-correction, that very same individual begins to experience **success!** The healing agents chesed and gevurah train you to avoid trying to fix, and instead to focus on desirable behaviour only.

You are taking a mighty stand by refusing to give away your precious energy in response to negativity, but with God's help, you will witness clear evidence of healing within mere *days*. You will be able to actually track the miraculous transformations as they unfold. Master the steps of this dance, and healing is in your hands.

Summary: Gevurah = "I can disconnect at will!"

Tiferet—Compassion/Beauty

Tiferet is the sixth sefirah and the third healing agent. It derives from the "centre," the seat of compassion and beauty. "On the third day God uncovered the dry land and gathered the water into oceans, seas, rivers and lakes. He covered the land with vegetation."

On the third day of Creation, two separate things occurred. First, the water was gathered into distinct bodies, revealing dry land. Second, the land was covered with vegetation. Like the third day of Creation, the sefirah of tiferet involves two distinct interventions. One of these enhances chesed, the other clarifies gevurah. Likewise, tiferet has two meanings: **compassion** and **beauty**.

Compassion

After a few days of experiencing the pure, clean energy of "I see you" and the contrasting disconnect that follows negativity, it's time to bring a bridge of **forgiveness** into play. Once children (and adults) experience what clean energy feels like—and also what a clean withdrawal of relationship feels like—there comes a desire for permission to try again.

Compassion—in this context—is allowing a person to experience the feeling of having a clean record.

Tiferet is the synthesis of chesed and gevurah. It is forgiveness in action. In video games and sporting events, the time-in (play) and brief time-out (penalty) are almost seamless, with the focus always on **time-in.** Someone breaks a rule, gets a quick penalty, and then jumps right back into the game. This is precisely how tiferet works.

After a few days of disconnecting without warning in response to a broken rule and then reconnecting without explanation (gevurah and chesed respectively), it's time to introduce code words to provide clarity and forgiveness (tiferet).

First, introduce a code word that is designed to sound the alert that a line has been crossed or that a rule has been broken. Keep your voice and body language calm and free of emotion. You could use one of these or make up your own: Freeze. Pause. Cut. Stop. Reset. Red light. Chill. U-turn. Oops. Try again. Take five. Use any word you like but use it *instead* of any other response.

I use the word "Reset" exclusively. It's clean, clear, and it doesn't sound punitive. It's what we naturally do when we err and want to try again, and it's what we do when an appliance malfunctions. The word "Reset" simply informs the person that a rule has been broken. Now the rule-breaker has been gifted with a choice: should I *continue*, or should I *stop*? You assist by staying emotionally detached and unavailable (offline) until the negativity stops.

You still need to turn away from the person once you have used the code word, as it can be hard to do the right thing when you are being watched. Not turning away puts him in an uncomfortable position. He may want to reset himself, but not want to lose face. By turning away after saying "reset," you are offering the gifts of **space** and **trust.**

The moment the rule breaking has stopped, use another code word to inform him that he has been forgiven. The broken rule is history, and he now has a clear record again. There is no need for him to apologize or ask forgiveness. Insisting on either one will undo all the progress you have made in a flash. These "courtesies" actually take the focus *off* success and shine the light on failure and energy for failure!

Here are a few code words to choose from, or again, make up your own word: Play! Go! Thaw! Come back! Green light! Roll! Welcome back!

I use "Welcome back" exclusively. I have found that it clearly conveys **compassion** and **forgiveness** without any hard feelings or residual effects. Within a minute of saying "Welcome back," validate the person with an "I-see-you" statement to confirm that the incident is history. Now and always, success is the only thing worth focusing on!

Tiferet is the perfect way to follow the advice of King David in Psalms 34:13–15: "Who is the man who desires life and who loves days to see good? Guard your tongue from evil and your lips from deception! **Turn away from evil and do good**, seek peace and pursue it!" This little piece of advice encapsulates the ideal way to promote healing.

This is how the sequence should flow in practice:

David has just done something wrong.

1. Look in his general direction and say, "**Reset, David,**" in a clear but emotion-free voice.
2. Turn away. Remain disconnected until the negativity stops. This usually happens within two to five seconds.
3. Turn back and say, "**welcome back.**"
4. Turn away *again* to give him the space he still needs to reset fully, and also so he doesn't get the feeling that you're challenging him. Continue with whatever you are doing for five to fifteen seconds. This gives him time to refocus.
5. Look straight at David and say, "**David, I see that you** are right back on track now! You have calmed yourself, and you are right on

task!" (Replace this statement with any other statement that is relevant and nourishing.)

6. Turn away *a third time* to give him space to digest this piece of information and so that he will not be tempted to prove you wrong.
7. Within a minute or two, engage fully with a generous validation which fits the scene.

Here's the tiferet flow in sequence: "Reset"—*turn away*—"Welcome back"—*turn away*—"I see you"—*turn away*—"here's what's happening now". Take particular care that you always articulate the person's name and the words *reset, welcome back* and *I see you.*

As soon as he—or anyone—has become accustomed to, and relatively comfortable with being reset in this way, step 4 can be skipped and steps 3 and 5 blended. At this point you would have a five-step flow, sounding like this:

Reset, David…

Welcome back, David. I see you are calm now…

David, I am really inspired by your ability to let it go and refocus yourself so effectively! Look how quickly and seamlessly you conquered your anger!

(Of course, the "…" means turn away: once for just 3-5 seconds, then for 20-30 seconds.)

It is common and quite okay to feel an enormous emotional charge when you are being challenged by a difficult child or adult. If you need to calm (reset) *yourself* after giving someone a reset, use the time between "welcome back" and "I see you" (step 4) to breathe into your heart centre for ten to fifteen seconds before proceeding. Then thank her for calming down, backing down, or being back on task. Use chesed (I see you) to let her know what's going *right* in this moment.

When the reset is over, it's quite possible that the problem has not been resolved. In such a case, don't allow yourself to fall into a *hidden trap* by demanding compliance or apologies. **Don't get into a battle of wills!** It's *not* compliance that you really want, but rather an environment that is conducive to healing.

If something still needs to be done, allow the person the space to take the initiative to do it by leaving the room, or at least moving away from her and engaging with something or someone else. Be careful that you don't end up demanding compliance. You don't want to run the risk of ending up back at square one. It's not worth it.

Let it go, and after some days (or possibly weeks) she will naturally begin to take responsibility on her own. If the job gets done or appropriate action is taken, apply chesed. Let her know that you really appreciate her decision, and respect and admire *her* ability to let go, as well as her show of initiative.

The space you create when you turn away during a reset creates a vacuum. In time, this vacuum will become the catalyst which will enable the child (or adult) to begin to hear his inner voice, or *conscience*. As long as that critical space is filled with noise, the quiet conscience cannot be heard.

This explains why people don't generally learn from their mistakes when they are reprimanded, criticized or punished. They feel like they have already paid for the "crime" they committed and are therefore free to offend again.

Your inner voice is your internal compass. It will guide you to act in accordance with your core being if the right environment exists to hear it in the first place! This applies to anyone: children, adolescents, college students, colleagues, your boss, even your elderly parents!

Summary: Tiferet = "Let's play!"

Beauty

Tiferet also means **beauty**. Another function of tiferet is the beautifying of chesed, the primary "I-see-you" intervention. This aspect of tiferet gives profoundly healing information to the person you are addressing; information that works on clearing the *blockages* that have accumulated over time.

I want to stop for a minute to talk about "blockages". Earlier in this book you were introduced to Johnny and Samantha, children who were significantly "disabled" due to the inaccurate processing of information they absorbed and incorrectly interpreted when they were too young to challenge it. They both heard *well-meaning* cautionary advice, which they wrongly assumed to be accurate character assessments.

Once these children *believed* they were lacking in a particular character trait or ability, they simply stopped using it. They unconsciously put it to sleep! This is unfortunately a common phenomenon. It can be compared to the technician in a switch-room who discovers a switch that is malfunctioning. He simply flicks it off, thereby disabling it. A child who has unconsciously disabled switches which control important behaviours and functions has—what I like to refer to as—*blockages*.

Another analogy which can be useful is that of the *plumber.* A plumber is called out to repair a blocked drain. How does he do it? By employing an instrument which enters the drain and locates the material which is blocking it. The appliance then removes the material, leaving the drain clear and functional again. The next intervention works exactly like the electrician and the plumber.

You are now going to learn how to *beautify* your observations. Continue using the words "I see you", but now begin adding specific information about the *worthy choices, values, and skills* that are being demonstrated. This is fun, creative, and fool-proof intervention for tackling the tricky job of clearing blockages and enabling switches.

Here are some examples:

- David, I see you taking tiny pieces of material and making a pattern on your collage. You are showing such creativity!
- Hannah, I can see you waiting really patiently for your turn on the swing. Good for you!
- Mike, I see that you are really upset, but you're holding yourself together. You are using awesome self-control right now!

- Debra, it must have been so frustrating when you found your classroom such a mess, but you didn't take it out on your students. Instead, you showed remarkable forbearance despite your disappointment!
- Danny, you are carefully walking along the balancing board. You are so focused! You're concentrating hard and stretching your arms out for balance.
- Mariana, I see you thinking hard, taking your time, and showing perseverance!
- Zoe, thanks for stopping to help Noa. You're being kind and patient.
- James and Peter, **I just caught you** cleaning up the classroom when you thought I wasn't looking! You are really considerate and responsible students!
- Mike, look at how you just threw that paper right into the bin! You have good aim and awesome coordination!

In the above statements, the following values were pointed out: creativity, patience, self-control, forbearance, focus, concentration, carefulness, balance, thinking, perseverance, kindness, patience, consideration, responsibility, aim, and coordination. These words describe qualities we want to **grow**. We grow them by noticing them and pointing them out!

When we wax poetic in this way, we have our *timing* right. We are teaching skills and values when the recipients are most receptive to learning—*when they are being successful!* This is also when they are most open to hearing and accepting our validations, because we are *catching them in the act!*

By providing undeniable *evidence* of their skills, abilities, values, and achievements as soon as we notice them, we provide valuable information and insight into who they really are! And the best part is that a juicy observation takes *only a few seconds!*

Adults are fixated on teaching values to children. That's great, except that they often choose the very **worst** times to teach those values. Children are most receptive to instruction when they are being *successful*. By pointing out values when you see them happening, you are offering three gifts:

- noticing when things are **not** going wrong
- providing valuable information which will help discard debilitating labels and replace them with more accurate and healthy ones
- honest appreciation

We pick up values quickly and easily when we are "caught" demonstrating them. This is especially true when someone struggles with a particular quality such as honesty, patience, responsibility, or kindness. By pointing out such qualities when such a person is **demonstrating** them, he or she is able to take *ownership* of them. Children are able and very willing to *discard* all sorts of labels when they are confronted with concrete evidence of their successes.

In contrast, when we try to teach values or skills when they are lacking, the child gets a plateful of *emotional junk food* instead of the emotional nutrition she really needs. In addition, she is getting:

- a failure experience
- evidence that supports existing labels or serves to create new ones
- clear evidence that she is more visible and far more interesting—even *lovable*—when she makes a poor choice

None of these will motivate a child to change. Quite the contrary! Tiferet empowers adults in the same ways it heals children. They too begin to heal and become emotionally stronger when they are presented with evidence of their qualities and values.

Try this exercise: Read the following statements and rate them with one of the following codes: **EJF** (emotional junk food) or **EN** (emotional nutrition).

- I just noticed you picking up the pieces of food that you dropped. That was very responsible of you.
- Stop following me around everywhere. Find something constructive to do.
- Stop whining. I will be finished soon.
- I see that you can't do that on your own. I'm coming to help you in a minute.
- I can't believe this! I leave the room for less than three minutes, and I return to find the toys away, and the cushions off the floor! You are incredibly capable and efficient!
- I said *no*! Why are you arguing with me? You are so argumentative!
- You really want that treat. You're upset that you can't have it, but you are handling your feelings in a mature way.
- Anna, you are in too much of a rush. If only you would slow down, you would get more of those problems correct.

Now try this: Look at the statements you coded **EJF**. Use the space below to turn them into **EN.**

____

____

____

____

Creating Pathways

It is human nature to focus on what's going wrong. Adults are very quick to notice what needs fixing in children's behaviour, and also in the behaviour of other adults. We take offense easily, we bristle at someone else's lack of consideration, get huffy when our children whine or are impatient, and we simply boil when we see injustice!

It's *great* to turn away from negativity when it happens rather than engaging with the "offender," but it's even *greater* to find a way to **transform** those annoying or worrying habits into *successes*. Tiferet is a brilliant way to do just that! When you notice that a child or adult has a particular weakness or bad habit, make a mental note of it. Then plan a *pathway* to create success and healing. Here's how:

Do you want to teach patience to Steven? Find a moment to say, "Steven, I see you waiting patiently while I finish up here!" Don't wait for Steven to get impatient. You jump in first!

You want Sarah to be less aggressive? Find opportunities to say things like, "Sarah, I just noticed how you were so careful not to step on Wayne's fingers while you were climbing the ladder with him. You are really looking out for his safety!" Don't wait for an "accident" or *incident* to happen.

You want Joy to dawdle less in the mornings when you're in a rush? Try, "Wow, Joy, look at you! You have both your socks on already! You are being so co-operative this morning!" She may move slowly, but focus on her progress. That way she will be motivated to be more on track.

You just hate it when Billy whines the entire afternoon? Try statements like, "Billy, we've been home for a while now, and you have been happily playing with your cars. You are being super calm today!" Again, *don't wait* until he loses it.

It's possible that these children are actually making an effort to change. If so, it's important to honour their efforts with your attention. Even if the lack of negativity is not deliberate it soon will be.

Adults are no different. They desperately need and crave recognition for their efforts. When people *of all ages* hear these kinds of statements, they begin to see themselves differently. They are getting all the information they need to discard labels they may have been wearing almost all their lives! Change your focus. Keep seeking opportunities to notice when things are going *right*! Or even better, when they're **not going *wrong*!**

Summary: Tiferet = "Look what's going *great* right now!"

On a Roll

You are now conversant in six of the ten sefirot. You are well on your way to personal and communal healing. You may even be beginning to **enjoy** this challenging but transformative journey. It makes a lot of sense, it's empowering, and it works! You may also be enjoying the fact that your family is more relaxed and calm, your students are now buying into success, and your work environment is more pleasant. Whatever your personal findings are, you are still reading, still learning and still engaged. That shows tremendous commitment!

The next phase of your journey will bring you to a level of mastery. The true master has signed up to a lifelong commitment to learning, practicing, and moving forward. Once you are in touch with your soul, you are in touch with infinity. That is the place where learning and growing; and discovering your unique and incredible potential never stops. You are now ready to learn and master the last four healing agents: netzach, hod, yesod, and malchut.

Welcome to the next empowering phase of your journey: **mastery!**

Mastery

The last four sefirot are the culmination and completion of the creative—and healing—process. Even now, before you master netzach, hod, yesod, and malchut, you are actively taking responsibility and doing your part in healing yourself and the world. God is with you. You are important to Him. What you do matters!

Netzach is victory—learning to master your innate desire to rebel. Hod is splendour—learning some very powerful "tricks" to empower and heal. Yesod is foundation—the discovery of the pivotal and fundamental reality and power of **now**. Malchut is sovereignty—the last piece of the puzzle, the final healing agent that will ready you—and the world—for redemption. Together, these sefirot will enable you to see yourself and the world in a totally different light, and to find your unique way to capitalise on that awareness.

Netzach—Victory

Netzach is the seventh sefirah and the fourth healing agent. It derives from the "right," the side of kindness. On the fourth day God created the sun, moon, and stars. On the fourth day of Creation, God caused the sun, moon, and stars to be the primary providers of physical light and warmth on Earth.

The entire universe prostrates itself to God. Each day the heavenly bodies all raise themselves up but ultimately bow in submission to their Creator. We humans have also risen higher and higher in our own estimation through the generations, but perhaps we are finally ready to humble ourselves before our Creator. This is the ultimate victory, because it's only our exaggerated sense of entitlement (self) and of our own importance that distracts us from becoming the **awesome** beings we were created to be!

True victory is when a person humbles himself before his Creator to the extent that he chooses to serve Him with his entire being, willingly offering up his will to do God's will. Global victory is when the entire human race willingly serves the One God as one being with one heart. This is not impossible. In the year 2448 after creation, an entire nation numbering around three million people achieved just such a state of unity when they received

God's word at Mount Sinai. When humankind is aligned with its purpose, true unity is inevitable.

Like the fourth day of Creation, the fourth step in the healing process is **conquering** our innate desire to rebel. Netzach is learning the art of **rule keeping**. God gave just seven commandments to the descendants of Noah. That's all. Boy, are we having a hard time keeping them! Adam was given only *one* commandment and couldn't keep it. **Why?**

Have you ever seen any creature of land, sea, or air, any size, colour, or shape **ever** not complying with its God-given mission in life? Have you ever heard a dog or a monkey or a fish; a mosquito, plant, or mushroom say ***no***? **What about the sun, moon, and stars?** Powerful as they are—hey, people have worshipped *them* since the beginning of **time!**—they submit to God on a daily basis. They would never dream of rebelling against their Maker!

Netzach is teaching rules in a way that guarantees children and adults alike will learn them *and keep them* with almost no effort at all! It is also incredibly effective in ensuring people don't "**forget**" the rules. Like tiferet and its fail-safe way to teach **values** when they are being demonstrated, netzach is all about teaching **rules** when they are *not* being broken!

Here is what netzach sounds like in practice:

- Harry, I see how mad you are at your brother, but you are not hitting or kicking him!
- Amanda, you could so easily have ignored my request for help, but you complied willingly!
- Brad, you knew it was supposed to be your turn on the computer now. You made the choice to be patient while Ella finished off her game. You didn't lose your temper with her, and you showed tolerance.
- Jake, I see you making several attempts at working out those problems. You're not giving up, you're not falling apart, and you're not cursing. You are staying calm, focused, and determined!
- Hey, Mike, you're really mad at me right now. You could have yelled at me, run away, or even hit me, but you didn't do any of those things! You are handling your anger in such a mature way!
- I see everyone in this room working quietly, you are all in your seats, and no one is disturbing or distracting anyone! You're keeping all the classroom rules!

- David, you're disappointed that supper isn't ready and the table isn't set. I really appreciate your tolerance. You could have let your frustration out by yelling at the kids or me, but you chose to just find a spot on the sofa with a drink and a newspaper while I finish up. Thanks for that!
- Danny, thanks for using an "inside" voice! Steven, thanks for walking down the hall and not running. Michelle, thanks for making sure you're not late for class! You are such responsible students!

For some odd reason, people are generally afraid to show appreciation for rules not broken. Whether this is because they feel it sounds negative, they are afraid of putting "ideas" into someone's head, or for some other reason, I have noticed that many people initially find this healing agent difficult to engage with. Once they overcome their resistance however, they are unfailingly delighted with the sheer creativity and power of this intervention!

As you can clearly see from these examples, **appreciation** is the key to teaching rules. Teach rules by showing appreciation when they are being adhered to, which is any time they are *not* being broken! When children are taught rules in this way, they are **motivated** to keep them because they are being acknowledged for their efforts and for already being **successful** at keeping them. They naturally begin *loving* rules ***and*** **compliance**!

Summary: Netzach = "Hey, thanks for not breaking the rule!"

Hod—Splendour

Hod is the eighth sefirah and the fifth healing agent. It derives from the "left," the side of Restraint. On the fifth day, God created the fish and birds. There is little that is more splendid than the breathtaking variety of different creatures that inhabit the oceans, rivers, lakes, and skies. The host of distinguishing features, habits, and ingenious tricks and practices they have been endowed with for survival and procreation is simply stunning! Each living creature was created absolutely successful and absolutely brilliant!

Like the fifth day of Creation, the fifth step in the healing process is creating a conducive environment for every single person you interact with (including yourself, of course) to positively shine. This is no longer just about appreciating values and rule keeping; it's about refusing to accept the notion that anyone is anything other than **magnificent**.

Birds are distinguished from other creatures by their ability to fly, fish by their ability to swim. Hod is the healing agent that will give you the ability to fly and swim, and to enable others to do the same. Flying is about overcoming obstacles. Swimming is being immersed in turbulent waters, yet being free, buoyant, graceful, and loving it!

Hod gives you the power to create success by cleverly manipulating what you see and reflecting it back as an aspect of a person's splendour. Hod is refusing to allow anyone to fail. It is a set of practices that *tricks* people into success. Hod is a catalyst that impels some of the most troubled people on the planet to admit that they too are worthy. It allows them to live productive, happy lives by compelling them to finally believe in themselves enough to discard the debilitating labels they have become so "comfortable" with.

Success isn't some distant, difficult, or unachievable goal reserved for some elite class; success is anything that isn't failure! And **failure is the stuff success is made out of!**

Hod is a set of three tricks cleverly designed to create success where it wouldn't be likely to happen on its own.

The first trick

When you want something done, don't say please! Say one of the following:

- Mike, **I need you** to take out the trash now.
- Sandra, **it's time to** come inside.
- Marsha, **you need to** get ready for bed.
- Pam, **it's time to** get up now.

The word **please** implies that there is a choice to comply or not to comply. Use unambiguous language when something needs to be done. Make your instructions sound like instructions and not like invitations to debate, ignore, bargain, or procrastinate.

On the other hand, if you are making a personal request, then please is the right word to use. For example, you might say:

- David, can you please get me a glass of water?

- Mika, please let Elana use your green cup.
- Briana, can you please cover for me for five minutes?

The second trick

When it looks like someone is about to break a rule, reflect back the intensity of the feelings he or she is experiencing, then truthfully say what rule could have been broken but hasn't been broken (yet). Say something like the following:

- Wow, Julie, you are so mad at Hannah! You could have smacked her or pushed her, but you are hanging in there and holding that anger! Now *that's* **healthy** power!
- Jerome, you obviously do not agree with me at all, but you're holding your peace and not arguing. I appreciate that!
- Donald, I just caught you stopping yourself from throwing that book! Now **that's** restraint!

Don't worry if the person breaks the rule anyway; just give a quick five-step reset. But nine times out of ten, you will have skilfully crafted a success where it would not have happened on its own. Such "tricks," designed to head off failure, create highly nutritious alternatives to "Don't you **dare**!" or similar warnings. The latter is a challenge, a failure experience, an energy trap, and **rarely** stops the person anyway.

The third trick

Count **steps toward success** as successes in their own right. Imagine calling the children inside for supper or after recess. If any child even looks up, you have something to celebrate. If anyone moves toward the door, you have a lot to celebrate! Focus on **steps toward compliance** and you will find plenty of emotional nutrition to enthusiastically share around. Here, the trick is to focus on what's going *right*, and simultaneously *refuse* to energize what's going wrong.

Here's what you might say:

- Kids, time for dinner! … Josh, I see you looking up from your game! You're being really attentive! Amanda, I see you saving your work! Simmy, you're on the way to the door already! You kids are being so co-operative!
- Kids, we're leaving in fifteen minutes! … You are totally focused today! Josh, you

have finished your breakfast already! Amanda, you have packed your backpack and remembered your homework! Simmy, you have found your shoes!

- Sandi, I see that you're almost ready. The kids are in bed, you're dressed, and you're putting on your make-up. Thanks for being so sensitive to my desire to be on time!

Handling frustrating situations and difficult transitions in this way transforms the atmosphere in the classroom, workplace or home. Instead of feeling pressured, negative, and stressful it becomes synergistic, focused, and goal-oriented. Instead of everyone feeling tense and the atmosphere becoming harried and unpleasant; joy, accomplishment, and deep gratitude are felt. Instead of handing out emotional junk food, hod allows you to deliver buckets full of emotional nutrition!

Tricking children into success

You are fully aware that trying to gain co-operation or teach values and rules when things are going wrong is a waste of time and counterproductive.

Here's something else to consider: Every human being **intrinsically** knows right from wrong and knows how to behave appropriately—*even very small children!*

When you teach children rules and values, you are not teaching them anything new. People are **born** knowing right from wrong. This innate, intrinsic knowledge comes from our very essence: being good and being kind is as natural and fundamental as breathing. Do children (or adults) really **forget** basic rules and values? Do they forget to pick up after themselves, to use a fork or to say please? If not, why do they seem not to know or to forget the rules so frequently?

Because it **pays**. People get more juice out of life from adversity. Howard Glasser aptly calls this phenomenon *upside-down energy*. Small children learn this truth long before they can think, and therefore, understand their motives. By the time a child is able to think, nurture has overtaken nature. The need for relationship has overridden the need for justice. Children just *know* that life would be so **boring** if they kept all the rules all the time. They would be virtually invisible!

We human beings need two *fundamental* ingredients in order to thrive: **approval** and **relationship**. Most of us are forced to choose between the two. This is where hod comes into play. When we learn to interact with others in a way that *both* these ingredients are abundantly available at all times **except** when negativity is happening, we begin to heal. We begin to care. We begin to hear our conscience, and we awaken to our true, Godly natures.

Some standard practices in our society seem to trigger a bout of forgetful or oppositional behaviour. Hod is a simple set of tricks that helps us avoid these triggers and simultaneously promotes successful outcomes.

The first trick

When an adult asks a challenging child anything using the word please, that child takes it as an invitation not to comply! The child might not say no outright, but she won't do what you ask either. The child will either pretend she didn't hear you or say something like, "Soon," or, "In a minute"—and then conveniently "forget" what you asked her to do.

When something needs to get done, you need clarity, not politeness. If you use the words "I need you to," "You need to," or "It's time to" before making your request, the likelihood of you gaining compliance skyrockets! You don't need to use a forceful or harsh tone of voice; just mildly say what needs to be done and then calmly turn or walk away to give the person you are addressing the space she needs to comply without feeling that you are challenging her to a game of "upside-down energy" (energy for negativity).

The second trick

By jumping in and "accusing" a person of being successful when he is about to break a rule, you are simply tricking him into success instead of allowing a failure to reinforce his belief that he is not in control of his actions. The truth is that when you **hijack** someone in this way, the person is **still** free to break the rule, and is still free to fail. You are just helping him out by giving him the "excuse" he needs to be successful against formidable odds. You are creating new pathways, but old habits can die hard. You are simply lending him a helping hand.

The third trick

By celebrating steps toward success, you are making it crystal clear that the **only** thing you are interested in and the only thing you are going to celebrate is **success**! You are like the bells and whistles on the computer game that encourage players all along the way, and not just when they have passed a level. You are like the spectators at a sporting event who constantly cheer when players are moving in the right direction, and not only when they actually score.

Then, when the person has successfully completed the task or chore required, or has successfully disengaged from an intention to break a rule, reward him with your focused relationship in the form of genuine appreciation. Be sure to heartily acknowledge each incremental step toward self-mastery. Go ahead and wax poetic! Now is a great time for a lecture about what **didn't** go wrong!

If you apply hod or any of the other healing agents and the person breaks a rule nonetheless, give her a quick five-step reset and then energize her for calming herself or for not breaking the rule again (or another rule). For example, "Joanne, *I see* that you're experiencing strong emotions. I appreciate that you have stopped yelling and have calmed yourself."

If she still refuses to reset, let it go. She will soon realize that she would much rather succeed than fail for two fundamental reasons:

1. Energy, connection, focused attention, and success experiences are only available in response to compliance and choosing wisely.
2. In the vacuum that is created by a brief reset, she will begin to hear her inner voice, which until now was inaudible.

Ultimately she will make a pivotal discovery: “I don’t like how I feel when I don’t do the right thing.” This realization is the beginning of true healing, which is not likely to happen if we don’t create that essential “void” by removing our energy from the equation.

Fish and birds

All creatures great and small utilize tricks, talents, gifts, and innate qualities to survive and thrive. That’s how they were created! And so were you! As you become skilled at using hod along with the other healing agents, you will notice something begin to shift in the way you see yourself and others, and in the way others begin to value themselves. You, your children, spouse, extended family, friends, and co-workers, will all begin to swim, dive, surf, fly—and soar! Success will be the norm, good choices the most likely and common outcome, and emotional healing will become unavoidable!

Summary: Hod = “I’m not just swimming, I’m *flying*!”

Yesod—Foundation

Yesod is the ninth sefirah and the sixth healing agent. It derives from the "centre," the seat of compassion and beauty. "On the sixth day God created all living beings that walk the land." A person's yesod is his or her basic nature. Animals are characterized by passion. Our "animalistic" drives are our passions.

One way children differ from adults is that they have yet to tame their passions. Taming and harnessing our passions is what distinguishes humans from animals, and what distinguishes adults from children.

[There are many adults who—due to neglect, abuse, or other causes during their formative years—were never able to emotionally mature. These adults need not despair. With these healing agents, time, and practice, they can—with God's help—attain happiness, confidence, self-respect, control of their lives, and become contributing members of society.]

All the myriad creatures that inhabit the earth have one thing in common: the only time that truly exists for them is **now**. Animals do not stress about the past, nor worry about the future. In this, children are similar to animals: the only thing that concerns a child is *now*.

All animals are programmed to utilize the *now* for getting their needs met in the best way possible. They do not choose freely; they choose what option serves their needs best at any particular moment. They choose the best spot to build their nests or dens, they choose the most promising mate from the selection available, they choose the safest route to food or water, and they choose the most nutritious option on the breakfast menu.

They don't choose to eat or not to eat; they eat when they are hungry. They don't worry about their next meal when their tummies are full unless they are programmed to do so. Their choices are not real choices; they are the smartest option from the animal's created perspective.

Yesod is the healing agent of **living in the present** and making the wisest choice at any given moment. Only when our worries and fears about what happened in the past or what could happen in the future are put aside are we truly free to make a choice. By living in the **now**, we are able to cleverly manipulate the future *and* the past to create and to *become* healthy and worthy citizens.

Yesod is a perspective of forgiveness. It allows people to be imperfect and to grow from their imperfections. It is an aspect of compassion. A compassionate person will create an environment where people can move forward. Yesod is a manifestation of trust. You show your faith in a person when you refuse to extrapolate into the future or perseverate in the past, where failure has occurred or might occur.

Yesod is the foundation of healthy living. It is truly living in the present. It is refusing to bear a grudge or to take revenge or to shame a person for past transgressions. Yet it is holding up that very same person to the highest of standards, with the expectation clearly being that the failure that just occurred will not occur again.

This is what yesod sounds like in practice:

- David, you amaze me! You are so disappointed and hurt, but **right now** you are refusing to get stuck in negativity. You are using all your power to stay focused and solution oriented!
- Dana, thanks for giving me the space I needed to calm down. **Right now** you are holding your peace, and that is helping me be able to focus on finding a solution.
- Shane, I see you **in this moment** finding your schoolbag, locating your homework, and being totally focused and responsible!

- Michelle, you could have so easily lost it just now, but instead, you are utilizing **this moment** to curb your fury at your sister and refuse to lash out at her! You are using incredible restraint!
- Daniel, **right now** you are not arguing with me or yelling at me. I really appreciate that!

Every time you capture a moment in time with the potent healing agent of yesod, you manipulate the past by learning from it and correcting it; you manipulate the future by being better prepared for it; and you enhance the present by creating a refreshingly new and exciting reality. With yesod, you become a time traveller: you change the course of history!

Yesod is so incredibly powerful because it allows you to grow what you want to grow and starve everything else in your inner garden. **You** decide what you want to keep and what you will discard. You become a connoisseur, a gem collector. You can capture any moment in time and transform it into a miracle! By zooming in on what's right in any given moment, you are able to expose the deepest qualities in yourself or in another person. You can find within that moment any and every quality and bring it out into the open where it can be truly appreciated.

We are accustomed to the exact opposite of yesod. We are continually faced with reminders—courtesy *ourselves* (primarily) and others—of where we are falling short! These constant reminders just undermine our feelings of self-worth, and *grow* the very qualities we want to starve!

Yesod means "foundation". The foundation of mental health is truly appreciating your myriad qualities. With yesod, you can explore and find priceless treasures hidden in the very deepest recesses of your own—or any other person's—soul. And everything you uncover is an aspect of who you really are! It is part of your passion, your essence.

Man was created in God's image. That means that we *all* possess spiritual qualities without limit. Every time you highlight one of these qualities, you expose it to sunlight and grow it. With yesod, you become a creator. You create goodness, kindness, patience, compassion, diligence, and countless other values or spiritual qualities simply by identifying and exposing them in a single moment in time!

Summary: Yesod = "This is the brilliant quality I discovered in you right now!"

The Tenth Sefirah

Up until this point, you have learned how to heal yourself and others using six potent spiritual healing agents. You are about to learn about the seventh and final healing agent, *malchut*.

Malchut is the crowning glory of all the healing agents. It is the glue that holds all the others together, and the ultimate fuel that powers personal and global healing. The entire universe was created for man, and man was created to establish a fitting home for God in this lowest, physical world. Malchut is the final healing agent that makes this possible.

Earlier in this book, I briefly introduced Adam Kadmon, supernal man. The ten powers and three garments of your soul mirror those of Adam Kadmon. These powers and garments are how the soul expresses itself. Here is a quick recap:

The "head" of Adam Kadmon (chachmah, bina, da'at) represents the soul's thought. The "torso" (chesed, gevurah, tiferet, netzach, hod, and yesod) represents the expressive/emotional powers of the soul. These are termed "speech." The "legs" (malchut) represent action. Thought is the soul's private domain. Speech relates to others, the soul's public domain. Action impacts the entire universe.

Malchut is the birthing of thought and speech (emotion) into action. Action relates to the world. Our **behaviour** is ultimately what we are responsible for. Our actions define who we are. They determine whether we are *building* a home for God in this world, or *destroying* it. Malchut is action—**mastery**.

Welcome to the action phase of your journey!

Malchut—Sovereignty

Malchut is the tenth sefirah and the seventh healing agent. It derives from the "centre," the seat of compassion and beauty. "On the sixth day God created the land animals … (and in the late afternoon) God formed Man from the earth and breathed a living soul into him … On the seventh day God rested."

Animals are characterized by raw emotion and passion, man by reason. Emotion is hot and seething; reason is cold and calculated. Animals use reason to satisfy their desires; humans are supposed to use reason to **control** them. Malchut represents a fusion of the two: passion harnessed by reason, plus reason enlivened by passion.

Malchut is the culmination of the creative process. It is the catalyst that causes the purpose of Creation to become manifest. It's like a switch that causes all the wiring hidden in a building to actively fulfil its purpose. Malchut—the seventh step in the healing process—is the consolidation of all the healing agents that preceded it. In practice, malchut is **responsible leadership**.

Each day of Creation parallels one thousand years of the world's existence. On September 14, 2015, the universe celebrated its 5,776th "birthday," so we have officially entered the fourth quarter of the sixth millennium. The seventh day, the Sabbath day, is representative of the seventh millennium, the Messianic era. Just as the Sabbath is welcomed in the late afternoon of the sixth day—the time of Adam's creation—the Messianic era will arrive in the latter part of the sixth millennium—any day now!

God commanded Adam to be fruitful and multiply, to fill the Earth and rule it. God gave humans the awesome responsibility of being the stewards of our planet. Adam's first initiative was to gather all the animals together to prostrate themselves to God, their Maker. Likewise, it is our task to submit the "animal" within ourselves to the service of our Maker.

It is interesting to note that Rosh Hashana—the New Year—is celebrated on the sixth day of Creation, and not on the first. This is because man is the purpose of creation. Adam was the catalyst who originally set the world as we know it into motion, and very soon his descendants will usher in the era of redemption. *Willingly or against their will.*

The Messianic era is the time when the lion will dwell peacefully with the lamb, when swords will be converted into ploughshares, and when evil and illness will cease to exist. The seventh millennium is the time when God will reveal Himself to humanity, and we will all serve Him as one. We will have no desire for evil; no desire for anything other than to know God. It's time for humankind to prepare this lowly and imperfect world to become a fitting dwelling place for God.

The two qualities that complete the healing process are *humility* and *gratitude*. These qualities are critical to being an effective leader. Moses—the greatest leader of all time—confronted Pharaoh and prevailed. He led three million Jewish slaves through the desert and formed them into a powerful nation with the Code for the survival *and redemption* of the universe. Two of the outstanding qualities Moses possessed were *humility* and *gratitude.*

Humility and Gratitude

Healing begins and ends with humility and gratitude. The Twelve Step Alcoholics Anonymous program centres around the admission that we cannot heal or help ourselves without the help of a Higher Power (God). It is only when we are able to acknowledge our utter dependence on a Power much greater than ourselves, can true healing begin.

The Torah attests to the fact that Moses was the most humble person who ever existed. Moses was not unaware of, or in denial of his greatness, but he was acutely aware that all his awesome greatness was nothing but a **gift**, and a reflection of God's Greatness. A truly great person is one who is humble and self-effacing in the extreme, yet acutely aware of his or her ability, responsibility, and mission in life. A truly humble person possesses one quality above and beyond all others: gratitude. True greatness is nothing other than *gratefulness*.

The Torah goes into some detail when recounting the creation of man for good reason: to grow and nurture the qualities of humility and gratitude. Man was the last being to be created; even the worm was created before him. Adam—the first human—was created from earth. Even the name Adam (translated as *man*) is derived from the word *adamah*, meaning "earth". He was created with the understanding that he comes from dust and will return to dust at the end of his life, like the rest of creation. The human being's life begins as a "putrid" microscopic drop, and will end as dirt and maggots. But for the grace of God, who gifted us with life, we are nothing.

Our true worth is measured not by how much material wealth or honour we accumulate, but by what we manage to *accomplish* during our lives in the service of God and humanity. Our value lies not in what we have, but in what we **give**.

Malchut is walking humbly with God and man. It is being careful not to demand, expect, or even *desire* kudos, respect, or honour. Humility is holding your peace, developing compassion, and avoiding anger. Anger comes into being from the thought: "How does this person dare do that to *me*?" It constitutes a subtle form of *idol worship* because in essence it is a denial that what happened is from God and with purpose.

Even if we are genuinely wronged by someone, it is the will of God. The individual who wronged us is culpable, but what happened to us was God's will. Malchut is the ability to accept God's will with humility, trusting that whatever happens to us is actually for our own benefit.

Happiness

Humanity spends much of its time as a species seeking happiness. No other creature on Earth or in the heavens has such a problem. It is interesting that having nobody to anger us, nothing to bother us, and being able to satisfy our desires does not lead to happiness at all—quite the opposite! It is humbling ourselves before God and giving to others that make us happy. We were *born to serve.*

Gratitude is the awareness that we don't have any rights in this world, only responsibilities. We are responsible first and foremost to ourselves. We are obligated to take care of our own physical, emotional, and spiritual health and wellbeing. We do not own our bodies; they were loaned to us by our Creator, to house our souls. Our bodies are the means by which our souls find expression. We need to treat our bodies with respect and care because they actually belong to God!

We are also responsible for the people, creatures, and planet we share. Our responsibility to others begins with our children and spouses and then extends to the rest of the world in the following order: our families, relatives, friends, co-workers, communities, cities, and countries, and finally the health, welfare, and safety of our planet and all of its myriad inhabitants.

And we are responsible to God. God gave us life as a gift, but in order to fully appreciate this gift, we need to give our lives back to Him. When we dedicate our lives to our own needs we are never happy, because our animal souls are insatiable! When we dedicate our lives to the service of God and humanity by meticulously observing the Noahide Code, we are automatically happy, because we were *born* to serve!

The opposite of gratitude—and happiness—is *want.* It is neither gracious nor healthy to be wanting. Avoth 4:1 has this to say: "Who is wise? He who learns from everyone. Who is mighty? He who controls his own nature. ***Who is rich? He who is happy with what he has.*** Who is honoured? He who honours others."

Humility and gratitude go hand in hand. When you are truly grateful, you are automatically humble; when you are truly humble, you are automatically grateful. Only when you are giving, forgiving, humble, and grateful can you be truly happy. When you forget to be grateful for what is going right, you default to being miserable, fearful, and angry about what is going wrong.

If you have an expectation that people do the right thing, but you forget to express *appreciation* when they do, things will start to go wrong. And your ego is ever-ready to jump right in with righteous indignation: "How dare you? How could you? Why did you? Why didn't you?" And so on. You end up insatiable and **miserable**!

Mastery

Malchut is mastering your nature by surrendering your will to conform to God's will (Avoth 2:4). But how does one become appreciative, humble, slow to anger, and quick to forgive? *By growing our self-control* through employing the healing agents. Self-control enables us to harness the incredible power and energy of our animalistic drives and emotions to **serve** instead of demand. Self-control is the master which tames the animal within each of us.

Self-control is a spiritual muscle. Just like your physical muscles, the more you use it, the stronger it gets. If your actions are primarily a result of what your animal soul dictates, your animal soul gets stronger and controls your behaviour. If you train yourself to act in accordance with the dictates of your Godly soul, then your Godly soul becomes stronger, and you become better and better at controlling your passions, drives, and desires. With practice and vigilance, you can harness your passion and your energy for a higher purpose. Your *actions* are the critical factor, because the way you behave defines who you are and who you will ultimately become.

Adam was commanded to rule over the world—including the animal kingdom. Likewise, every one of us is continuously summoned and challenged to master our own small world: our own unique set of emotions, passions, and animalistic tendencies and drives within us. To truly heal, we must constantly exercise our spiritual muscles with the aid of the ten healing agents.

Your self-control is not the entire picture. In order for you to become a true master of your actions, you must possess both humility and gratitude. You also need to develop a constant awareness of God, who watches your every step and your every move. He is *literally* right by your side at all times, ready to aid and assist you. He is *not* a God of vengeance, unless you are out to deliberately *defy* Him and to *cause others to err.* You need only to acknowledge Him. You will not always succeed—because you are human—but *failure is the stuff success is made of.*

Malchut in action

Malchut is not a set of things to say as are the other healing agents; it is the underpinning that enables you to use all the other tools effectively. The more you practice employing humility and gratitude in your everyday interactions, the more you grow these qualities. Use the words "thank you" often. Use every opportunity you can to show your gratitude, and—equally important—to swallow your pride. At first neither will be easy, but with *practice* they will become second nature.

With humility and gratitude, lots of patience, practice, and the constant awareness that you are not alone, you will be able to gracefully and successfully employ all seven healing agents to heal yourself and others. All the healing agents require you to master your emotions. Humility and gratitude make that possible.

Summary: Malchut = "Thank you God for guiding me. As insignificant as I am, I am changing the world one choice at a time!"

You have now graduated Part 2. Welcome to Part 3—The Humble Servant!

Part 3

The Humble Servant

A Guide for the Warrior

The Humble Servant

The King's Feast

There was once a king who made a feast for all his ministers. The king spared absolutely no expense to make sure that each minister would be able to partake of a mind-boggling selection of plentiful, luscious, and extravagant delicacies and beverages without restriction.

All of the king's ministers were of course invited to this feast, as were the important and distinguished servants of the king. All were seated comfortably at the king's own table, with a host of servants of lower rank serving them.

Although the feast was intended for the ministers, the distinguished servants also sat at the table. In addition, the servants and waiters and the entire staff of the palace were treated to everything they desired, even though the feast was not intended for the benefit of these employees of lower rank and status. The gardeners, butlers, guards, coachmen, and even the stable boys feasted. Even the lowly servants and chambermaids partook of the leftovers to their hearts' desires, although they were obviously not at the king's table.

Under the table were the dogs. Even these munched happily on the bones and scraps until they had all had their fill.

The analogue

The entire created universe—the heavens and the earth and all their hosts—is the King's table. The ministers are the ministering angels through whom God controls the world. The servants are those who are aware of God's existence and consciously serve Him. The dogs are the scavengers.

The ministering angels are the highest in rank, as they are closest to the King. They are in a constant state of trembling and awe before God, because they have a keen awareness of His awesome majesty. They serve God in a state of absolute self-nullification. *They do not possess any independent power.* The error of the early generations was the belief that these angels possess independent power, and can choose to bestow or withhold influence.

The servants can be subdivided into two general categories: the important servants, and the lowly ones. The important servants are those people who choose to serve God willingly, because they are wise enough to discern Him within creation, and they desire a relationship with Him. The lowly servants also serve God, but for ulterior motives. Perhaps they want to go to heaven and certainly don't want to go the other way; or they want to be repaid with a good life in this world. They also have a relationship with God, but it's more like a business arrangement.

The "dogs" are not concerned with the King at all. They will grab whatever is thrown to them without a thought for the *Giver* of all the bounty they enjoy. The moral fibre of the dog is dictated by its belief system. If it values life, it will protect life. If it doesn't (other than its own) it will put the lives of others in jeopardy without thought or conscience.

Even the category of dogs can be subdivided: those that think ahead, and those that don't. The dogs that think ahead are the cautious ones. They don't break the law, because they don't want to be caught and have to pay the consequences. They may, however, attempt to *change* the law to suit their purposes, if they can get into the right circles.

Those that don't think ahead don't plan ahead. They live in the *now,* but in a totally self-absorbed, self-serving way. They *literally* take whatever they want and do whatever they want, as long as they think they can get away with it. They have no shame, no fear, no sense of justice, and no sense of responsibility to others, no moral code except for their own.

The worst of the dogs are those who believe–or *pretend to believe*—that they have the needs and best interests of society and the world at heart. They are devastatingly misled—and they misinform and mislead the masses and the most vulnerable among us—to make choices that could literally undo the entire fabric of society, if God were to allow them to carry through with their evil schemes.

The Humble Servant

There is one person who sits at the king's table who hasn't been addressed yet: the humble servant.

The humble servant has only one desire: to be with the king. He is not interested in the food, the entertainment, or the opulent setting. Instead, he sits at the table and fixes his eyes on the King Himself. All he wants it to be at the King's service. He only wants to *please* the King. He would give his life for the King without a moment's hesitation. He has no sense of self at all: his whole focus—his whole *life*—is only to fulfil the will of the King.

And the King too has only one desire. The King's eyes scan the cavernous banquet hall. They take in the ministers, the important servants, the lowly servants, the staff of the palace and the dogs. And then they lock with those of the humble servant. The King has found what He was looking for. *This* was the true purpose of the feast.

THE WARRIOR

The Spiritual Workout

Personal and global healing is all about self-mastery. We tend to think of fighters, commandos, ninjas, rabble-rousers, gangsters, terrorists, politicians, the rich, and the famous as the strong and powerful people in our society. They are not. They are God's tools for His revelation, or for His hiddenness.

The mighty warriors in this world are those who vigilantly monitor their emotions and refrain from *reacting*, choosing to exercise restraint and to respond wisely and thoughtfully instead. They assess their every move and every response before they act, and use their intellects to deduce the best response in any given situation.

This does not mean that they don't have feelings or emotions. The emotions of a true warrior are just as intense as anyone else's. The difference is in their ability to stop and think before they act.

Using your intellect and your power to choose your course of behaviour and responses is as difficult as exercising or working out. A person who spends 90 percent of his or her day at a desk job and the other 10 percent in slow motion will undoubtedly find exercising excruciatingly difficult to begin with. But with persistence and determination, any exercise routine designed for that person will become easier. If she stays committed to a more active lifestyle, in time she will undoubtedly regain her strength and flexibility. It's all about training, determination, and perseverance. And training some more.

The same principle applies to any worthwhile undertaking: learning to respond appropriately is all about priming and toning your emotional muscles. The result of an intensive programme like this one is a new lease on life. You will feel liberated, happy, focused, fulfilled, and valued. You will have found true contentment. You will have discovered clarity.

Once you taste from this tree of life, you will want to share your inspiration and success with others. You will have the internal motivation and wisdom to continue on a path of healing and Divine service on a communal and perhaps even on a global level. You will become another potent healer for humankind and for the world.

Tohu and *Tikkun*

Before this physical world was created, God created many spiritual worlds and destroyed them, because their "light" was too powerful for any "vessel" to contain. These worlds are collectively referred to as *tohu*. Tohu represents unbridled power. In this world, tohu manifests itself as a malevolent, destructive force. The work of harnessing tohu is referred to as *tikkun*. We all experience a taste of both tohu and tikkun in our lives and in the world.

When an individual is utterly overwhelmed, he experiences a taste of tohu. When he experiences relief, he tastes the world of tikkun. Insanity comes from the world of tohu. So do natural disasters. So does evil in any shape or form, as do war and sickness. The antidote to tohu is tikkun. Tohu is spiritual darkness. The antidote to darkness is light. Tikkun is that light.

The Spiritual Sources of Human Emotions

Emotions come into being from the seven sefirot, as all of creation does. Here is a list of the sefirot and their corresponding emotions, both harmful (from tohu) and beneficial (from tikkun).

Chesed, *negative character traits*:

Wastefulness, frivolity, lust, overindulgence, non-compliance.

Chesed, *positive character traits*:

Kindness, thoughtfulness, generosity.

Gevurah, *negative character traits*:

Anger, pride, cruelty, jealousy, harshness, inflexibility, stubbornness.

Gevurah, *positive character traits*:

Restraint, practicality, patience, discernment.

Tiferet, *negative character traits*:

Unreliability, confusion, indecisiveness, boastfulness.

Tiferet, *positive character traits*:

Compassion, honesty, clarity, forgiveness.

Netzach, *negative character traits*:

Pushiness, bigotry, stubbornness.

Netzach, *positive character traits*:

Decisiveness, self-assuredness, focus.

Hod, *negative character traits*:

Frivolity, pettiness, vanity.

Hod, *positive character traits*:

Aesthetic awareness, creativity, class.

Yesod, *negative character traits*:

Self-absorption, stinginess.

Yesod, *positive character traits*:

Calculating, honesty, goal-oriented.

Malchut, *negative character traits*:

Pride, indifference, haughtiness, aloofness.

Malchut, *positive character traits*:

Regal bearing, leadership qualities, grace, self-respect, responsibility, maturity, proactivity, insightfulness, self-control

The Road to Self-Mastery

Planning your healing regimen

Now you have everything you need to begin your healing regimen and to progress steadily from level to level of achievement. Of course, you can simply use the seven healing agents as prescribed in Part 2 of this book, and you will undoubtedly experience profound healing, equanimity, fulfilment, meaning, and joy in your life. But you can also be a warrior. You can choose to create a more streamlined, specific regimen of healing for yourself, based on your personality, qualities, and tendencies. You can achieve this by using the information presented here to create your own tailor-made programme to achieve self-mastery.

Using your natural emotions and responses as your base level, you can learn to manipulate your tohu (negative or destructive) emotions and transform them into tikkun (positive and beneficial) emotions by substituting them with an alternative from the same family. Then you can systematically grow these qualities with the seven sefirot as outlined above.

Here is an example of how this works:

Imagine that from 7:00 a.m. to 8:30 a.m. on the average weekday is a difficult time for you. No matter how great your intentions are, every morning leaves you feeling frustrated, exhausted, and lousy. You can't seem to use the healing agents consistently or effectively during this time period.

Take the time out now to identify the emotions you feel and the sefirah or sefirot that birth these emotions. Now substitute these emotions for closely related emotions of healing and growth from the same sefirah. Revel in your new power and self-control as you slip into a new role of mastery. Rejoice in your new image. Watch the magic when things just refuse to go wrong!

"I have identified fear of chaos as a prime catalyst in undermining my good intentions in the mornings. I have a natural tendency to overly control my environment, and difficulty with trusting that other family members are capable and focused. I tend to assume that they don't want to be organized, and this expectation of failure works against us all. I have identified my negative emotions as fear, distrust, and despair. The sefirot involved in my negativity are tiferet and yesod.

"My healing regimen is going to be taken from the sefirot my negative emotions stem from. I will use my knowledge and my trust to transform these 'tohu' emotions into 'tikkun.' I will convert my fear into excitement, forgiveness, and trust. I will replace my failure self-talk with compassion, honesty, and goal-focus from tiferet and yesod."

Using beneficial emotions from the same family and sefirah as substitutes for our harmful ones is easier and far more useful than trying to squash or fight them. Forward planning is the key to success. By identifying and modifying your emotions, you are creating a pathway for true and lasting growth and progress. This simple formula can be used to convert any negative, ingrained patterns of behaviour to beneficial ones.

Think about people who irk you or set you off, places that make you feel awkward, hostile, or incompetent, times of the day that overwhelm you, patterns of behaviour in yourself or others that put you into a tailspin. Apply the above principles for three to five days to create new neuron chains of growth and power within yourself.

Fear and Trust

All negative emotions are ultimately based in fear (the left side of Adam Kadmon), and all positive emotions are ultimately based in love (the right side of Adam Kadmon). But fear and love are not opposite emotions. The opposite of love is hatred; the opposite of fear is trust. The antidote for all negative emotions is **trust**. All adversity and difficulties are put in our path to challenge us and help us grow. You *can* successfully deal with them, with **trust**.

Fear is the quintessential point of tohu, and trust is the quintessential point of tikkun. So go ahead and heal yourself. Go and heal the world! Use all the healing agents as prescribed, but keep the foundation in your pocket at all times: trust that God is right by your side, right now and always, to aid and assist you on your journey. Bon voyage!

Back to Basics

The Spiritual Workout

Let's now revisit the Noahide Code with our new knowledge and understanding. I want to point out that each one of these "laws" is a general category, and includes a subset of laws. This is not the place to go into all the particulars of the laws, but books are available which do. See *Recommended Reading* on page 165.

These are the general categories of laws which comprise the Noahide Code:

1. **Believe in God**
2. **Reject idolatry**
3. **Do not murder**
4. **Do not steal**
5. **Do not commit adultery**
6. **Do not torture any creature**
7. **Set up law courts**

Believe in God

Belief in God is fundamental to healing. When you know without a doubt that your life has meaning and that you are accountable to a Higher Authority, you can *really* live in peace with yourself and others.

Take your belief in God to the next level. Don't think of God as irrelevant to your life or as an entity totally beyond your experience and reach. Don't waste time struggling with questions that lead you around in circles. I'm referring to questions such as, "Does God exist? And if He does, does He still maintain interest in our lowly world? Does He know I exist? Does He really care what choices I make in life? Is there really reward and punishment? Why do good people suffer and bad people prosper?"

All of these questions just distract you from connecting with your deepest self. If God can create an entire physical universe as well as countless spiritual worlds, He can take an interest in you too. He invested His creative energy into making you the unique individual you are. You did not pop off an assembly line, He *invested* in you. Now it's your turn to invest in Him. You only need one commodity: **trust**. Educate yourself, do your best, and trust that He will help you set and reach your goals. The Lubavitcher Rebbe said, "Your birthday is the day

God decided that the world cannot exist without you." It can't, and you wouldn't want it to, either!

Belief in God is synonymous with **chesed**. By investing in a lifelong partnership with God, you are demonstrating pure kindness to God, yourself, and the world.

Reject idolatry

Idol worship is essentially the erroneous belief that there is anything in existence other than God that has the ability to control your internal or external environment. It is also the belief that anything or anyone can *obstruct* the will of God, including you.

Everything that occurs in this world is absolutely by design, and everything you encounter has been presented to you for a specific purpose. If you were to use your free choice to harm or harass, you would incur guilt upon yourself, weaken your Godly soul, and strengthen your animal soul. Still, you would *not* have interfered with the Divine plan in any way. If God "let you get away with it," it was meant to happen. If God didn't want it to happen, your plan to harm would not have succeeded.

Rejecting idolatry is the quintessential embodiment of **gevurah**. It is the mindset of turning away from negativity, rebellion, anxiety, self-doubt, and blame and categorically refusing to use anything as an excuse to be less of a person than you were born to be. Face up to what is on your plate and master it!

Do not murder

This fundamental law is a very worthwhile standard to use in assessing the true nature of belief, religion, politics, societies, the world, and life. Not taking a human life is one of the seven basic laws of humanity for good reason: Any person, government, political force, nation or religion that employs or condones murder to achieve its ambitions or goals is anti-God and evil by definition. True belief in God and murder are mutually exclusive.

Not to murder is **tiferet**. It is the act of having compassion and mercy, working *with* life and humanity instead of against it. It's wrong to kill *anything* without good cause, such as for fun or for sport.

On a subtler level, don't kill means **don't waste**! Murder is the tragic waste of human life, but in a sense, wasting time, valuable resources, food or water are all subtle forms of killing.

Do not steal

Train yourself to trust that everything that happens to you is for your benefit and growth. You will no longer covet another person's possessions once you have internalized the fact that God gave you exactly what **you** need to fulfil your life's purpose. Want (jealousy) is the opposite of happiness. Trust and **appreciation** for what God has given you create happiness.

Whether you want to steal a penny or a car is immaterial; stealing is rebelling against your Maker. If the object you want was meant for you, it would already be in your possession. Anything that is meant for you already has your "name" on it. Nobody can it take away from you. If something of yours was stolen, it wasn't *meant* to be in your possession for the long term. If it was, you can be sure that it will eventually be returned to you.

Do not steal is **netzach**. It is conquering your desire to have what someone else has, and being victorious over your natural inclination to believe that you should have more than you have been given.

Do not commit adultery

A marriage is blessed by God. Cheating on your spouse is defiance of the will of God, and will not bring you happiness or contentment. Controlling your desires, vigilantly guarding your fidelity, learning to really, truly appreciate **your** spouse—who was created just for you—and being the best life partner you can possibly be will bring both of you true love, companionship, happiness, and fulfilment. Do not commit adultery is **hod**. It is a glorious, beautiful path to personal and global fulfilment and completion. Nobody is perfect, but a couple who faithfully enhance, support, and complete each other is as close as we can get to perfection.

Do not torture any creature

The actual prohibition is tearing a limb or body part from a creature for food while it is still alive. Doing so creates a cruel and heartless nature. Any kind of pain inflicted on any creature on earth without good reason is classified as cruelty, and as such, it opposes God's will. Slaughtering an animal for food must be done in the most humane way possible (hence, the fastidious laws of "kosher" ritual slaughter).

Causing needless pain or distress to any living being is forbidden. If it is in order to improve the creature's overall quality of life, the pain should be minimized to the greatest degree possible. Embarrassing or shaming people is akin to physically abusing them, and is therefore also forbidden.

The world was built on kindness. Not hurting is the encapsulation of **yesod,** foundation. Remember that you were born by the grace of God. It is only fair that you show your appreciation by respecting and caring for your co-creations to the best of your ability. The essence of a worthy, meaningful life is being sensitive to the needs of others, and responding compassionately to a fellow creature's distress.

Set up law courts

Unfortunately, people generally do not take God, life, or their personal obligations to humanity and the world seriously. People tend to do as they please, simply because they can. God commanded us to set up courts of law, so the fear of the law and of being caught would ensure that society would not revert to tohu, chaos.

Take a hard look at the place where you live. Do the citizens in your country live in relative safety?

Wherever the Noahide Code isnot enforced nobody is truly safe. In places where they are actively flaunted, society degenerates to anarchy. We have seen this happen countless times through our history and even in our very recent history! Even today—well into the twenty-first century—there are some godless places where chaos rules.

Setting up courts of law is **malchut**. Malchut is sovereignty, majesty. The kingdom of Earth is meant to be a reflection of the kingdom of Heaven. In societies where there is responsible and effective enforcement of law and order, there is relative peace and prosperity. When the Noahide Code is embraced globally tohu will be utterly transformed into tikkun, and a majestic sense of peace and tranquillity will reign supreme. Jealousy, crime, hatred, warfare, poverty, and illness will simply cease to exist. The ultimate purpose of creation is for all seventy nations (all of mankind) to bring Heaven down to Earth by committing to observe the Noahide Code in its entirety. Let's make it happen. For our children.

LEGACY

To my children

A mother's heart is like a starfish. It gets broken time and time again, but with God's help, it mends itself over and over. It is also like the ocean. It can never run out of love and compassion. I love you all more than you will ever fathom.

I want to give you a legacy that is worth far more than the material assets that (to date) I cannot share with you. I want to gift you with a legacy of fulfilment, happiness, joy, and delight for ever more. I want to give you one asset that will provide you with the ability to meet all of your emotional needs. Please accept my gift of *Born to Serve*.

Happiness and fulfilment are simple (but not easy) to acquire, but necessitate letting go of a lot of *stuff*. When you finally permit yourself to let things go, you will find yourself free to swim, and to soar. You need ten essential ingredients. Here they are.

Keep them in your pantry and in your heart at all times. Ingest and digest them all frequently. Share them with your children, friends, and family liberally. And don't worry—it's impossible to overdose.

1. Chachmah. Know that your emotional energy is your greatest asset. Use it wisely.
2. Bina. You were born with a very unique and very intense nature. You can learn to harness its incredible power and use it to propel you to become the gift to the world you were born to be. I am still learning. It is a lifelong lesson.
3. Da'at. Trust in God. Study the Torah diligently—particularly Chassidut (the inner dimension of Torah, as taught by the Chassidic masters in general and the Rebbes of Chabad in particular), pray with devotion, and don't ever stop performing acts of goodness and kindness. If you undertake this journey and share its healing power, you will help transform the world.
4. Chesed. Your journey must begin with kindness. Learn to be kind to yourself and to others, especially those who are closest to you. They are the most difficult to be loving

toward, because they have the capacity to hurt you the most. When you give the gift of unfiltered kindness freely when nothing's going wrong, people will reciprocate in kind and things will go wrong less often and less significantly. Take the time to really see and appreciate the presence of others.

5. Gevurah. Learn to detach when something goes wrong. Master the art of resetting yourself. The rest will follow naturally and exquisitely.
6. Tiferet. Forgive quickly, freely, and genuinely. Develop your quality of compassion. Nobody is out to get you; people just get stuck in their own emotional whirlpools. Learn to forgive and move forward for your own mental health and happiness. Beautify your interactions by showing appreciation for the qualities evident in yourself and in others. Create pathways to healing by watering the flowers and not the weeds.
7. Netzach. Master the art of actively celebrating rules not broken. Honour yourself and others for your effort, and for the attainment of worthy goals and achievements. Make it a habit to appreciate

rules not broken, feelings not hurt, responsibilities not shirked, and time not wasted. This may sound silly, but it isn't. It is electrifyingly healing.

8. Hod. Step in and lend a hand to bring out the best in yourself and others. Use a pleasant tone of voice without sacrificing clarity. State what needs to be done, simply and clearly. Don't wheedle, beg, and supplicate. When progress is happening, celebrate it! Learn to trick yourself and others into success.
9. Yesod. Engage in the process of success, *right now*! Zoom in and discover priceless treasures buried within yourself and others at any given moment. Appreciate the wonder and beauty of every moment that nothing's going wrong, because each one contains miracles waiting to be discovered. Devaluate society's fixation on results and final products. The gift of life is in this very moment.
10. Malchut. Develop the qualities of humility, appreciation, and gratitude. These are the qualities that give you the ability to focus on the bigger picture, know your place in the world, and know how to become a true master and leader. Humility enables you to

hear your inner voice (your Godly soul) and to accept its guidance. Constant gratitude to God and honest appreciation of others keep you happy and healthy. Your true value is not in what you have, but in what you **give**. Malchut is mastery. In order to master anything, you need to work on it constantly.

Trust in God

Above all, remember that you have absolutely nothing to fear. Place your trust in God alone. God created you by design. He painted the masterpiece that is your life in all its finest details. Just for you, and just for the benefit of your unique soul. *Life is a journey, not a destination.*

Remember: you were born to serve.

You have no rights.

Here are your responsibilities, in order.

1. To God
2. To the Rebbe
3. To yourself
4. To your immediate family
5. To your relatives and friends
6. To your community
7. To your people
8. To your homeland
9. To your country of residence
10. To the world

God bless you!

Recommended Reading

Cowen, Shimon Dovid. *The Theory and Practice of Universal Ethics.*

Freeman, Tzvi. *Bringing Heaven down to Earth.*

Glasser, Howard, and Jennifer Easley. *Transforming the Difficult Child.*

Jacobson, Simon. *Towards a Meaningful Life.*

Rosemond, John and Bose Ravenel. *The Diseasing of America's Children.*

Taub, Shais. *God of Our Understanding.*

Weinberg, Rabbi Sholom B. *Healthy in Body, Mind and Spirit.*

Weiner, Moshe. *The Divine Code.*

About the Author

I am a teacher, mother, grandmother, and author. I have authored or coauthored several children's books, some of which have yet to be published. I have raised nine children together with my dear husband. Currently, I live in Melbourne, Australia, and I am a member of the Chabad community there. My guide and mentor is the Lubavitcher Rebbe, Rabbi Menachem Mendel Schneerson.

I was born in 1960 in Sydney, Australia, the second of four children and the first of three daughters. My parents provided a happy, warm home for us and sent us to small parochial schools for our education.

I was not an easy child. I dropped out of school at fifteen and trained as a teacher in Gateshead, England. At the age of eighteen, I embarked on a forty year and growing teaching career, a choice I had coveted since my early teens. In 2005 I opened my own "school," a home-education support centre for children and teenagers who were unable to thrive in mainstream schools.

In 2009 I was forced to close this much-needed institution due to the financial crisis of 2008. Almost all the thirty-three students who came for support and assistance went on to finish their education in mainstream settings and embark on satisfying careers or higher education. Some of these former students now have families of their own!

Shortly after my school closed, I was given a book to read that changed my life and ultimately transformed the lives of many families in crisis or struggling to stay intact. The book was called *Transforming the Difficult Child*, and the author was Howard Glasser. Much of what is written in this book is gleaned from the wisdom and writings of Glasser, and his renowned healing programme, the Nurtured Heart Approach.

I became a Nurtured Heart Approach (NHA) advanced trainer in 2010, and since that time I have had the privilege to be a catalyst for relief and healing to scores of families and individuals in Australia and abroad. I have provided NHA training for parents, educators, therapists, schools, and child care centres.

From the moment I was introduced to Glasser's healing programme, I recognized the correlation between his findings and the ancient teachings of the Kabbalah. In 2011 I created a healing programme based on the ten building blocks of Creation and the Nurtured Heart Approach, which became obsolete when the standardized Visual Training Module became available to NHA trainers.

It wasn't until a few years later—in 2015—that I became convinced that a more comprehensive guide was needed for a species in crisis: the human race. That was when I became obsessed with what I believe to be my Divine calling—to bring true healing to humanity and to the world with the ten healing agents and the Noahide Code.

Made in the USA
Monee, IL
31 March 2021